TWO IN THE FIELD

VIVIAN LENORE DILLARD

authorHOUSE

AuthorHouse™
1663 Liberty Drive
Bloomington, IN 47403
www.authorhouse.com
Phone: 833-262-8899

Published by AuthorHouse 12/17/2020

ISBN: 978-1-6655-1131-5 (sc)
ISBN: 978-1-6655-1130-8 (e)

TABLE OF CONTENTS

DEDICATION

Two in the Field is dedicated to the jewel hidden in the field, the remnant of God, whom I pray will be comforted and will have their faith and hope renewed by the writing of these words.

ACKNOWLEDGEMENTS

To my God, who marked me with love in my mother's womb, thank You for being my peace, my joy, and my hiding place.

To my husband and friend, my fellow Berean, thanks for supporting all of my spiritual endeavors.

To my children and goddaughter, thank you for continually pursuing God. You encourage me, and you are greatly loved by God.

To Bishop Howard A. Swancy, a champion for Christ, thank you for strengthening my faith and renewing my hope in waiting for the rapture.

To Dr. Johnny James, who makes everyone feel important in the Kingdom, thank you for listening to me and giving me a book that showed me how God reveals His word to me. Your assistance is invaluable.

To Shunna Foster-Bradford, thank you for reviewing this book and for giving me an "A."

IN MEMORY OF

Bishop Charles L. Taylor of San Diego, California, my father in the gospel who provoked me to be strong in the Lord, encouraged me to be sound in doctrine, and taught me that ministry begins at home.

Dr. Norma E. Jackson of Los Angeles, California, my mentor in Christ Jesus who taught about the Lord brilliantly, with clarity and passion.

Bishop Ross Paddock and Bishop Norman L. Wagner, profound leaders of the Pentecostal Assemblies of the World, Inc. whose gift of teaching constantly provokes me to search for a deeper understanding of the revelation of the Word of God.

Bishop William L. Smith and District Elder Elsie Eads of Los Angeles, California, two of the meekest pastors gifted to the body of Christ who unknowingly made me hunger for the Word in my youth, while they simplistically expounded on revelations in our fellowship meetings.

Bishop James A. Johnson, whose messages have strengthened me daily, especially "The Inflexible Directive." Thank you, Bishop, for giving me a clearer understanding of what it means to suffer for Christ

INTRODUCTION

Do you look at people professing to be Christian and ask yourself questions because, what you see them do contradicts what they say? Well, you are not alone. Even the strongest believer could become confused focusing on people in the visible church.

It is upsetting to hear that a leader or follower has fallen into sin or been overcome by evil; and it's worse to learn that a believer has taken their own life. Also, people are being deceived, falling away from the truth of God to turn strange doctrines.

If we look too long at the visible, we will get discouraged. Remember, Jesus warned His disciples about the last days so they wouldn't get discouraged. He told them the last days would be a time of deception by false prophets and false Christs. It would be so much deception that if it were possible, these false teachers who claim to be anointed would even deceive the children of God.

These are the last days. These are the days that Jude said mockers would come walking after their own ungodly lusts, separating themselves, being sensual, and not being sanctified by the Spirit. These are also the times that Paul called "perilous" when men, including ministers, would be lovers of themselves. These are the days that Peter said scoffers would question the second coming of Christ because nothing has changed since the beginning of creation (Matthew 24:24, Jude 1:18-19, 2 Timothy 3:1, 2 Peter 3:4).

We need divine understanding to walk in faith and have peace with God. Two in the Field is written to provide a step in that divine direction; including, taking your focus off of the visible church and putting it on the church that Christ built. Nothing is as it appears, with the natural eye: everyone in the visible church is not necessarily part of the church, everyone leaving the visible church is not, "fallen away," and all of Israel is not Israel (Romans 9:6).

Part I Worlds Apart

"The field is the world. The good seed are the children of the kingdom, but the tares are the children of the wicked one." Matthew 13:38

THE GREAT DIVIDE

It is widely accepted that Adam and Eve were separated from the presence of God because they sinned against God by eating from the forbidden tree. Based on the scriptures, Eve was deceived, and Adam willfully transgressed against God. The one commandment that he violated caused a separation or a great divide between God and man. This kept Adam, Eve, and their offspring from having access to the one tree that would have given them eternal life.

If Adam and Eve were created innocent, what could provoke them to go against the only command God gave them which would result in death? The answer is, they were corrupted by the introduction of another way of life — another doctrine or teaching. Where there was one teacher, now there are two. There was another message besides the words of eternal life that God had spoken unto Adam in the garden where they communed daily.

Because Adam and Eve had willingly embraced this other way, a way that seemed right, they were divided and could no longer boldly commune with God.

No one can fully appreciate the devastation that without divine understanding. This transgression was no small thing — it caused a great divide, for no man could have access to the tree of life except he die.

This divide made two worlds, while you only see one. It is like the gulf that separated the rich man and Lazarus. You look at the one place called hell, but there are really two places. There is no way a man could see, end or remove this type of separation (Luke 16:20).

> *"And beside all this, between us and you there is a great gulf fixed: so that they which would pass from hence to you cannot; neither can they pass to us, that would come from thence." Luke 16:26*

The gulf or "gape" in this parable is a fixed separation between the righteous and unrighteous who are dead in hell or the grave. The only way to end this type of separation between the two different abodes is through death—the second death.

> *"And I saw the dead, small and great, stand before God; and the books were opened: and another book was opened, which is the book of life: and the dead were judged out of those things which*

were written in the books, according to their works." Revelation 20:12

"And the sea gave up the dead which were in it; and death and hell delivered up the dead which were in them: and they were judged every man according to their works." Revelation 20:13

"And death and hell were cast into the lake of fire. This is the second death." Revelation 20:14

And again, God said…

"He that overcometh shall inherit all things; and I will be his God, and he shall be my son." Revelation 21:7

"But the fearful, and unbelieving, and the abominable, and murderers, and whoremongers, and sorcerers, and idolaters, and all liars, shall have their part in the lake which burneth with fire and brimstone: which is the second death." Revelation 21:8

The gulf will not exist after death; and hell are cast into the lake of fire because the righteous will have been resurrected and reunited with God for eternity.

Unbelief is a sin that separates people from God eternally. It is a dangerous road to travel! It's hard to have peace with a God you can't see or refuse to believe. False doctrine is another way that disrupts the harmony between God and man. Hearing and obeying false teaching caused the initial separation between God and man. It divided the minds of Adam and Eve and their hearts followed. They were divided because they saw and believed an alternate way of living in the paradise of God.

The devil was teaching in the garden of God. Who would've thought anyone could be so bold! What he spoke to Adam and Eve became an option. It was a lie, but still another way that was NOT like God said from the beginning. God gave clear directions for the first family to abide in the garden and have life. The alternative to what God said came from the Serpent; and with his doctrine came reward, and the idea that man could become gods. Some kind of lie this was. Deception so deep that it robbed Adam and Eve's peace with God. It was a great lie, but man was not the first to embrace it.

Satan, fallen Lucifer, was the first to attempt being a god or deity like the Almighty God. It was evil ambition! It provoked him into rebelling against the only true God, which was his creator. For this reason, God cast him out from the heavens and God's abode; and He removed Satan from his place and demoted him to roaming the earth.

Being dis-fellowshipped from God did not stop Satan from spreading his ideas and lies. Satan went on a journey to corrupt anyone that would listen to him; and seduce everyone to follow him and his ways. This is why he was speaking through the serpent. He was continuing the wicked message he initiated in the heavens, that anyone could be a god; and unfortunately, he has been very successful.

When Satan fell from heaven, he was not alone. One third of the heavenly host of angels employed by God fell with Satan. They believed the lie! I don't think they really knew the consequences of obeying sinful Lucifer. There is no enjoyable profit in disobeying God. You can't rise up against the almighty and have things go well you, or have a happily ever after. Satan lusted to be worshipped and adored as God. To fully walk in this type of authority, he would have to convince God's angels to follow him.

To validate his self-ascribed god-ness, Satan needed subjects. He needed followers to actually be worshipped. So being removed out of their place in the throne of God, one third of the angels fell into sin. The consequence of following Satan was eternal; and because they believed and followed his false ways, the fallen angels exist only to receive the great judgment of God.

> *"For if God spared not the angels that sinned, but cast them down to hell, and delivered them into chains of darkness, to be reserved unto judgment." 2 Peter 2:4*

> *"And the angels which kept not their first estate, but left their own habitation, he hath reserved in everlasting chains under darkness unto the judgment of the great day." Jude 1:6*

The angels willfully left their first estate! They abandoned what they were created to do. In leaving God they gave up their freedom. They were not free – they are not loose in the earth. Satan's only disciples was reserved in chains. Remember, you can't be worshipped without worshippers. Satan lost the angels he perverted, so he on the prowl. The wicked one is looking for new members.

Satan is recruiting others to follow him into darkness, this was really the only way Satan could prove himself as a god. Adam and Eve were his first earthly prospects. He taught them what they could do and showed them who they could become through the power of disobedience.

According to the serpent (that old devil that was in the garden of Eden), the reward of disobeying the true God would be greater than life. This false truth created a desire in them. The desire was great Eve, along with Adam, succumbed to the serpent's influence. They were filled with new desires, obeyed their ungodly thirst, and ate the forbidden fruit. All this to become as gods! It didn't work. When they consumed the fruit they became as dead men walking; for there is, and can only be, one God.

In the beginning of creation, it was evident who the Godhead was. Men lived by Him and were subject to Him; and all instruction came from Him. The godhead is not a mystery – living godly is.

> *"And without controversy great is the mystery of godliness: God was manifest*

in the flesh, justified in the Spirit, seen of angels, preached unto the Gentiles, believed on in the world, received up into glory." 1 Timothy 3:16

God did not create a substitute teacher for earth's first family; and He didn't give them alternative ways to live by. On the contrary, Adam and Eve were live by and teach God's words to their children. They were supposed to give the same doctrine and instructions they had received from God; and passing down these truths from generation to generation, would move each generation closer to God.

Before the serpent inspired man to rebel against God, man heard only wisdom speaking in the garden. It was the voice of the Godhead that spoke, "Let there be light" in the beginning of time. It was that same voice that instructed Adam to take care of God's creation. Sadly, the whispering voice of Satan was also heard in the midst of God's garden; and that voice, which is also the spirit of disobedience, continues to influence and coerce all creation to rebel against the living God.

"And you hath he quickened, who were dead in trespasses and sins." Ephesians 2:1

"Wherein in time past ye walked according to the course of this world, according to the prince of the power of the air, the spirit that now worketh in the children of disobedience." Ephesians 2:2

"Among whom also we all had our conversation in times past in the lusts of our flesh, fulfilling the desires of the flesh and of the mind; and were by nature the children of wrath, even as others." Ephesians 2:3

That spirit of disobedience, that is what provoked Adam to go against the command of God, and caused Eve to turn from truth. That same spirit is can be found working in every man, woman, boy, and girl that disobeys the commandments of God. It is not a new spirit, but an old spirit, one that motivates the innocents to reject God and follow their teachings.

Many people have been deceived by Satan. Some follow him willingly, and others ignorantly. Those that don't understand his influence, grow accustom to darkness; and often their way of life seems normal. Then there are other misguided souls, who reject righteous influence because they have grown fond of the dark.

"But if our gospel be hid, it is hid to them that are lost." 2 Corinthians. 4:3

"In whom the god of this world hath blinded the minds of them which believe not, lest the light of the glorious gospel of Christ, who is the image of God, should shine unto them." 2 Corinthians. 4:4

"For we preach not ourselves, but Christ Jesus the Lord; and ourselves your servants for Jesus' sake." 2 Corinthians. 4:4

The power of false doctrine is grossly underestimated. Take Adam for instance, because he yielded himself to obey the doctrine of Satan, his disobedient spirit has been passed on to every human born into this world. Everyone born in this world is born in bondage to sin. This is that sin nature that passes to all mankind through Adam's seed.

All of mankind has inherited the penalty that came with Adam's sin, but that does not have to be the end of the story for any soul. Anyone that turns their ear toward God and obey His commandments, can be freed from that eternal penalty; and will receive what Adam forfeited: access to the tree of life.

> *"Through thy precepts I get understanding: therefore I hate every false way." Psalm 119:104*

> *"Therefore I esteem all thy precepts concerning all things to be right; and I hate every false way." Psalm 119:128*

Adam's fall had a devastating impact on humanity. They had the ability to choose even in their innocent state of mind. Neither of them were acquainted with sin, or the evils that appeared as a result of their fall.

Eve was deceived in her choice to eat from the forbidden tree, Adam did it willfully. Whether by deception or disobedience, they both made a choice to something God commanded them not to do. They didn't know good and evil, but had power to refuse evil by doing good. If they had just did what God told them – that would doing good. They would have secured their access to the tree of life. But they made the wrong decision, and choosing to obey the wicked one, they sinned; and having that sentence upon them, there is only judgement and the wrath of God to look forward to.

> *"Ye that love the Lord, hate evil: he preserveth the souls of his saints; he delivereth them out of the hand of the wicked." Psalm 97:10*

> *"And this is the condemnation, that light is come into the world, and men loved darkness rather than light, because their deeds were evil." John 3:19*

> *"Let love be without dissimulation. Abhor that which is evil; cleave to that which is good." Romans 12:9*

> *"For he that will love life, and see good days, let him refrain his tongue from evil, and his lips that they speak no guile." 1 Peter 3:10*

The ability to choose to do good instead of evil is solely based on the revelation of God and His truths. Whether it is taught at home, church or revealed by the Spirit of God, a person can only walk in righteousness and truth when God gives an understanding of who He is.

> *"And this is life eternal, that they might*
> *know thee the only true God, and Jesus*
> *Christ, whom thou hast sent." John 17:3*

Eternal life is in knowing God and who He is. If an individual forsakes all that he is, all that he has, and walks in the revealed knowledge of the Word of truth, God will translate that dear one into His kingdom. In turn, that precious life will be preserved in Christ.

Tower 1: The Eternal God

"There is none like unto the God of Jeshurun, who rideth upon the heaven in thy help, and in his excellency on the sky." Deuteronomy 33:26

"The eternal God is thy refuge, and underneath are the everlasting arms: and he shall thrust out the enemy from before thee; and shall say, Destroy them." Deuteronomy 33:27

Imagine having such a relationship with the Almighty God, that at your cry, He rides up the heavens to help you in the time of need. It's possible! God is not only the Father of them that believe, He is the true Avenger! He is the preserver of life, and an eternal refuge.

The existence of every human being is dependent on God because, He is the creator of all living things great and small – the giver of life. There is, however, an opportunity for everyone to have a deeper relationship with God. A deeper relationship is possible through the revelation of God and Christ.

*"For this cause I bow my knees unto
the Father of our Lord Jesus Christ."
Ephesians 3:14*

*"Of whom the whole family in heaven
and earth is named" Ephesians 3:15*

Anyone desiring to be a part of the family of
God must be born again. This is the way to a deeper
relationship with God. This opportunity and door
comes at the preaching of the gospel – the call to go
deeper. If a person craves a deeper relationship, the
response to hearing the gospel will be to be baptized
in water; and wait for the baptism of the Spirit. Water
and Spirit – this is the way the identity changes, this is
regeneration. Out of the old family (Adam), and into the
new (Christ). Therefore, since the believers citizenship
is moved. The believer is translated from the kingdom
of this world into the kingdom of Christ.

All things pertaining to a believer's spiritual
identity is made new, and the believer is safe from
the wrath that will come upon the world because of
Adam's sin. This is why Satan has to seek for souls to
devour, because God has many souls preserved and
hidden in Christ.

Satan has to deceive God's elect in order for them

to come out from the protection of God. To do this, he does what he's been doing... lying. He seduces people by offering false security. And when these souls come out from under the shadow of God, he goes after them hard for the kill.

To claim the victory over Satan, and escape his trickery, is to test the spirit that is speaking by the scriptures, firmly hold on to the Word of Christ, and don't get entangled with teachings or behaviors that help you go back into bondage (Galatians 5:1).

Satan couldn't touch Job or the things he possessed, and he couldn't persuade Job to reject or fall away from God. The main reason Satan was unsuccessful in abusing him was because, Job dwelled under the shadow of the Almighty God; and Job continued to trust God's power to deliver.

This divine protection Job had, was and is the grace of God – that impenetrable hedge that Satan faced every time he tried Job. Job was safe with God! He believed and obeyed God, and therefore God counted Job perfect or complete in Him, or hedged. Though Job lost his family and friends, God was Job's refuge and help in trouble; and he put all of His trust and hope in Him.

"The name of the LORD is a strong tower: the righteous runneth into it, and is safe." Proverbs 18:10

Every born-again believer has this same assurance. If they believe on the Lord Jesus Christ and are born into the family of God, they are safe! This protection of God is promised, and is given to all that forsake themselves and their own identity to obtain the knowledge of Christ – and call God Father.

"Yea doubtless, and I count all things but loss for the excellency of the knowledge of Christ Jesus my Lord: for whom I have suffered the loss of all things, and do count them but dung, that I may win Christ." Philippians 3:8

Jesus also said,

"For whosoever will save his life shall lose it; but whosoever shall lose his life for my sake and the gospel's, the same shall save it." Mark 8:35

"For what shall it profit a man, if he shall gain the whole world, and lose his own soul?" Mark 8:36

"Or what shall a man give in exchange for his soul?" Mark 8:37

So then, God, the everlasting Father, offers all the security and substance that a good earthly father provides his children and more. It is all done in His name; and that is why all heaven in earth is named by that name. That is why every knee must bow to that name. That is why salvation is in that name. There is safety in no other name than the name of the Lord Jesus.

"But the Lord is my defence; and my God is the rock of my refuge." Psalm 94:22

Tower 2: Babylon

Ever since his heart was lifted up with pride, Satan has been violently trying to take over the kingdom of God. It began in the heavens when He tried to lay hold of the throne of God. Satan seized a moment and persuaded one third of God's angels to follow him in anarchy. Despite being expelled from the throne of God, Satan continues to seek glorification through exalting himself. He wasn't satisfied being the chief angel that glorified the Almighty, but rather, he worked to be glorified as god.

> *"How art thou fallen from heaven, O Lucifer, son of the morning! how art thou cut down to the ground, which didst weaken the nations!" Isaiah 14:12*

> *"For thou hast said in thine heart, I will ascend into heaven, I will exalt my throne above the stars of God: I will sit also upon the mount of the congregation, in the sides of the north." Isaiah 14:13*

> *"I will ascend above the heights of the clouds; I will be like the most High." Isaiah 14:14*

Satan, fallen Lucifer, trying to be higher than God is no small issue. Because of his prideful lust, the world has been turned upside down. His lust to excel above God was not and is not fulfilled, so, he is not satisfied; and he is not content with solely being the god of this world. He moves on mankind – working through them to experience his dreams and visions of dominance over all of God's creation.

> *"And then shall that Wicked be revealed, whom the Lord shall consume with the spirit of his mouth, and shall destroy with the brightness of his coming." 2 Thessalonians 2:8*

> *"Even him, whose coming is after the working of Satan with all power and signs and lying wonders." 2 Thessalonians 2:9*

> *"And with all deceivableness of unrighteousness in them that perish; because they received not the love of the truth, that they might be saved." 2 Thessalonians 2:10*

Many of the people God used to reflect His name in the earth, have been overcome by Satan. They moved by the same spirit that led Satan to his fall. That same spirit that was so wicked and out of control, that God banished it's carrier from the heavens to roam the earth: the spirit of pride.

> *"Pride goeth before destruction, and an haughty spirit before a fall." Proverbs 16:18*

> *"Better it is to be of an humble spirit with the lowly, than to divide the spoil with the proud." Proverbs 16:19*

> *"But Peter said, Ananias, why hath Satan filled thine heart to lie to the Holy Ghost, and to keep back part of the price of the land?" Acts 5:3*

The fall of most spiritual and world leaders, kings, and rulers, are due to lust for pride, power, or greed; and that includes those that had humble beginnings. It is becoming all too normal to read that a spiritual leader was removed from a church position because of immoral acts, or worse, crimes against family or church members. For those that wholly believe in the scriptures, these positions are ordained of God. If any leaders hold these beliefs, they should also have in their hearts the spirit of humility and compassion for others, to the point there are boundaries they will not cross – there are things they will not do. However, the sin of pride is powerful and has turned the heart of even the most humble.

"For the wrath of God is revealed from heaven against all ungodliness and unrighteousness of men, who hold the truth in unrighteousness." Romans 1:18

"Because that which may be known of God is manifest in them; for God hath shewed it unto them." Romans 1:19

"For the invisible things of him from the creation of the world are clearly seen, being understood by the things that are made, even his eternal power and Godhead; so that they are without excuse." Romans 1:20

"Because that, when they knew God, they glorified him not as God, neither were thankful; but became vain in their imaginations, and their foolish heart was darkened." Romans 1:21

One of the many historical and biblical figures used by Satan to take glory from God was Nimrod. At the start of his journey, Nimrod was humble. He became a mighty hunter because God strengthened him, and this might made him famous. His accomplishments also gave him confidence that fueled him to construct a tower that could reach the heavens.

> *"And Cush begat Nimrod: he began to be a mighty one in the earth." Genesis 10:8*

> *"He was a mighty hunter before the LORD: wherefore it is said, Even as Nimrod the mighty hunter before the LORD." Genesis 10:9*

> *"And the beginning of his kingdom was Babel, and Erech, and Accad, and Calneh, in the land of Shinar." Genesis 10:10*

He started humbled, but then Nimrod's heart was lifted up with pride and he was inspired to seek his own identity. This identity would be separate from God, who empowered Nimrod, and gave him strength to do all those mighty works. Does this sound familiar? It should. This is the same road Lucifer traveled—a crooked and wicked path to glory. While Lucifer was at his strongest and in the prime of his purpose, he sought an identity detached from his creator. One that gave self-gratification and vain glory. Babel was the product of such a spirit. All of Nimrod's works were before the Lord and gave God glory, until he became mighty, then he wanted to make a name for himself.

Satan thrives in confusion — He is the author of lies, confusion, and ungodly division. He provokes people to sow discord with the intent to divide and conquer. As if causing this type of chaos will make him a god – not so. God is one; and He alone was and is to be glorified as God. So, where did the confusion come from in Nimrod's vision?

> *"And the whole earth was of one language, and of one speech." Genesis 11:1*

> *"And it came to pass, as they journeyed from the east, that they found a plain in the land of Shinar; and they dwelt there." Genesis 11:2*

Clearly, God did not initiate this type of confusion because, from the time that God created Adam, until Nimrod set out to build his kingdom, there was only one language of speech in the entire earth. It was the language God gave mankind. There wasn't any confusion when all of the people were as one and began to travel from the East. The confusion started when Nimrod, and literally the whole earth, suspected their travels would cause them to be scattered. With Nimrod as their leader, the people conspired to build a memorial to preserve their name in the earth.

> *"And they said, Go to, let us build us a city and a tower, whose top may reach unto heaven; and let us make us a name, lest we be scattered abroad upon the face of the whole earth."*
> *Genesis 11:4*

Nimrod and his followers built a tower to commemorate their name in the land of Shinar, or ancient Babylon. What they did not go unnoticed. The Lord came down to see the city and tower.

> *"And the LORD said, Behold, the people is one, and they have all one language; and this they begin to do: and now nothing will be restrained from them, which they have imagined to do."*
> *Genesis 11:6*

Building the city and tower of Babel was not wrong of itself; it was the motive behind this construction that was questionable. The people were not unified to worship God like the patriarchs of old. Whenever Abraham, Isaac, or Jacob moved to a new place, they built an altar to give thanks and to worship the only true God. Contrastingly, Nimrod and the people came to a new land and built a tower to idolize themselves and be forever memorialized by their name.

The people that followed Nimrod were deceived by the same spirit that caused the rebellion in the heavens—that satanic spirit of fallen Lucifer, which also lusts to be memorialized (Isaiah 14:15). This deception exemplified the desire to exalt oneself above the stars to the throne of God. Instead of urging the people to remember the name of God, the people erected a memorial for their name to be remembered.

> *"Go to, let us go down, and there confound their language, that they may not understand one another's speech."*
> *Genesis 11:7*

> *"So the LORD scattered them abroad from thence upon the face of all the*

earth: and they left off to build the city."
Genesis 11:8

"Therefore is the name of it called Babel; because the LORD did there confound the language of all the earth: and from thence did the LORD scatter them abroad upon the face of all the earth." Genesis 11:9

THIS PRESENT WORLD

This present world, according to John's description, is comprised of three temptations: the lust of the eyes, the lust of the flesh, and the pride of life. The condition of this world was made known after the transgressions of Adam and Eve. Before their transgressions and disobedience, God's creation was good and walked upright. There was no confusion or chaos in the earth or its climate. There was harmony between God and man, and man and every living creature.

Before sin entered the world, man was at peace with the God, and had continual access to Him. However, because of Adam's sin, God was no longer accessible to man. Mankind no longer had the same spiritual liberties as Adam who walked and communed with God without sin in the garden of God. Mankind lost that privilege with God, and in order for mankind to walk peaceably with God again, man has to be transformed and become a new kind of creature — one that could exist in the realm of God.

From the beginning of creation, God has been revealing two natures of people in this present world; and these people are governed by two different kingdoms. One nature is obedient, being influenced by God, the spirit of holiness; and the other nature is influenced by Satan and the spirit of disobedience (Romans 1:4, Ephesians 2:2).

In the midst of this chaos, God gives spiritual knowledge to enlighten His people – to pull them supernaturally out of the darkness of this world. He equips them so they won't be distracted, and turn from the way that pleases God, and from following their course in this earth, which is to worship God only.

To help us understand the mysteries of the kingdom of God, Jesus gives us parables. In the parables of the kingdom of heaven, the field represents the world or the earth. God gives the revelation of these parables to help us know and maintain our identity in the earth. For example, when speaking plainly to His disciples regarding the kingdom of heaven, Jesus specifically defines the field as the world in His parable of the tares of the field (Matthew 13:38).

On the Mount of Olives, the disciples came to Jesus privately and asked Him questions regarding the signs of His coming and the end of the world. The first signs described the beginning of tribulation. Jesus spoke about the judgment to come and the increase of deception among the people of this world. Lastly, Christ explained how He would return and gather His elect from the earth. It was in His description of the state of the people during this time that Jesus reveals that there are two types of people in the earth (Matthew 24:36-40).

Jesus explained that His coming would be like the days of Noah when God destroyed all living creatures from the face of the earth. God would send this destruction because man's heart was increasingly wicked and their imaginations continually evil. Jesus also explained that upon His return to the earth some people will be obsessed with this life, and will not know that the wrath of God is coming until it's too late, and the church is taken out of the world (Matthew 24:39).

Jesus further illustrates the soon-to-be condition of the world by stating, "...then shall two be in the field." The two are not only two people, but two natures of people in the world. One nature will go after the things of this world, being governed by its lusts (Mark 4:19); and the other nature will seek after heavenly things, being led by the Spirit of God (Luke 12:31, Colossians 3:1).

Until the Son of Man (Jesus) sends the angels to gather His people from the four corners of the earth, these two will remain in the earth together (Amos 3:2-3, 2 Corinthians 6:17). These destructive days will be like the days of Noah when the floods divided the wicked from the righteous; and those righteous were the eight souls saved by the grace and mercy of God.

God does not reveal His secrets to everyone (Amos 3:7). The secrets of God pertain to godliness and eternal life, and this is what is revealed to the children of God, and revealed to those that obey His commandments. God makes Himself known to His people so they will be saved and worship Him in spirit and in truth (Deuteronomy 29:29). God doesn't want any to perish, He wants all of His people to be delivered from the wrath to come. The gospel is like the voice of God, it makes a distinct sound for those who have a spiritual ear to hear what God desires.

The church is defined in the Bible as a people who are chosen by God and sanctified in Jesus Christ. God elected the church in Christ in eternity before the creation of this present world. From Genesis to Revelation, God shows us that He intends to redeem the church from sin and the powers of this world. God will do this by His own determinate counsel; and by speaking to His people through Jesus Christ, teaching them the treasures of His kingdom in parables.

Parables are used in the Old Testament scriptures as well as the New Testament. They were spoken to declare the glory of God, to confound the wise of this earth, and to keep the kingdom of God hidden from unbelievers. Many believe that Jesus spoke parables to help the multitudes understand spiritual things more clearly, not so. The scriptures bear witness to the reason why Jesus Christ taught with parables. In response to a question from one of His disciples, Jesus answered:

"He answered and said unto them, Because it is given unto you to know the mysteries of the kingdom of heaven, but to them it is not given." Matthew 13:11

"Therefore speak I to them in parables: because they seeing see not; and hearing they hear not, neither do they understand." Matthew 13:13

"And He said unto them, Unto you it is given to know the mystery of the kingdom of God: but unto them that are without, all these things are done in parables." Mark 4:11-12

Jesus explained the kingdom of heaven in parables so that the children of this world WOULD NOT UNDERSTAND. This is contrary to the acceptable belief that Jesus used parables because they were easy to understand. I hope everyone reading this book fully understands this: To the church, a people that are not of this world, Jesus speaks plainly; and He opens their eyes to understand the will of the Father. You may think about putting this book down – to stop reading it. But read what Jesus said about how God hides His will:

> *"At that time Jesus answered and said, I thank thee, O Father, Lord of heaven and earth, because thou hast hid these things from the wise and prudent, and hast revealed them unto babes."*
> *Matthew 11:25*

God hides Himself from the proud heart. Maybe this is why there are so many versions of the Holy Scriptures. The scriptures cannot be understood by reading and studying only — they must be revealed or disclosed by the Author, God. The psalmist declared (by the spirit of God) that God would speak mysteries by parables. "I will open my mouth in a parable: I will utter dark sayings of old" (Psalm 78:2). These sayings refer to the Old Testament scriptures that the fathers and prophets of Israel sought to understand but could not.

> *"That it might be fulfilled which was spoken by the prophet, saying, I will open*

my mouth in parables; I will utter things which have been kept secret from the foundation of the world." Matthew 13:35

"Even the mystery which hath been hid from ages and from generations, but now is made manifest to his saints." Colossians 1:26

The parables of Jesus were not mythical tales, but allegories used to reveal God's will to His people, and at the same time hide it from the world.

"We will not hide them from their children, shewing to the generation to come the praises of the Lord, and his strength, and his wonderful works that he hath done." Psalm 78:4

ANOTHER WORLD

There are three basic meanings for the world in the Old and New Testament scriptures: 1) the earth and its inhabitants, 2) this life, age, or time, and 3) the church or kingdom of God. In the scriptures, world is most often used when referring to the earth or those that dwell in the land.

> *"Let all the earth fear the LORD: let all the inhabitants of the world stand in awe of him." Psalm 33:8*

> *"And spared not the old world, but saved Noah the eighth person, a preacher of righteousness, bringing in the flood upon the world of the ungodly." 2 Peter 2:5*

When Job said, "Man that is born of a woman is of few days, and full of trouble" in the 14th chapter, he was referring to man being born of this world, or this life. This is temporal. This is the world that Jesus said will pass away, and the world that Paul said will burn up with a fervent heat (Matthew 24:35, 2 Peter 3:10). For example:

> *"Behold, these are the ungodly, who prosper in the world; they increase in riches." Psalm 73:12*

> *"And they that use this world, as not abusing it: for the fashion of this world passeth away." 1 Corinthians 7:31*

Contrariwise, the church or age to come, speaks of a world that is eternal. To enter this other world, a man is reborn or translated out of this life (world) and into another world (eternal life) which is in Christ (2 Corinthians 5:17). This world is concealed in eternity, is perpetual, and it is not known to mortal man. It is hidden in God and only revealed to His children who are kept and preserved in Jesus Christ.

For example:

> *"But Israel shall be saved in the LORD with an everlasting salvation: ye shall not be ashamed nor confounded world without end." Isaiah 45:17*

"Unto him be glory in the church by Christ Jesus throughout all ages, world without end. Amen."

Ephesians 3:21

"But he shall receive an hundredfold now in this time, houses, and brethren, and sisters, and mothers, and children, and lands, with persecutions; and in the world to come eternal life." Mark 10:30

The scriptures define the church as a world without end. This church is made up of Jew and Gentile (Isaiah 45:17, Ephesians 3:21). This world is also a place and the power by which the church exists. Those who are called out of the natural world are transformed by the power of God's kingdom and translated into another world in God.

"Therefore say I unto you, The kingdom of God shall be taken from you, and given to a nation bringing forth the fruits thereof." Matthew 21:43

"Whether of them twain did the will of his father? They say unto him, The first. Jesus saith unto them, Verily I say unto you, That the publicans and the harlots go into the kingdom of God before you."
Matthew 21:31

"But if I cast out devils by the Spirit of God, then the kingdom of God is come unto you." Matthew 12:28

To connect us with our inheritance and give us hope in this life, Jesus reveals to us the mysteries of the kingdom of God. He uses pastors to feed us with knowledge and understanding of His Word, which first started with the apostles. This knowledge of Christ is eternal life, and those who reject the Word of God will perish (John 17:3, 1 John 5:20).

Being worlds apart from unbelievers, all of Christ's disciples believe on Him through the gospel or word spoken by the apostles. Therefore, believers are separated from the world by truth (John 17:17- 20).

The children of God are born physically as others into this world, yet are spiritually not of this world. Every believer has been predestinated by God unto the adoption of children. When they hear the preached word and are born again, they are translated from this world into the kingdom of God; like Mephibosheth, who was set in the kingdom of David to forever eat at the king's table (Ephesians 1:5).

By continuing in the apostles' doctrine, we openly confess that we are pilgrims and strangers in this present world (Hebrews 11:13). Like Abraham who went out not knowing where he was going, we look for our eternal resting place in the heavens because, this world is not our home. All that live Godly in this generation have this same testimony: one day Jesus will return in the clouds and catch us away with Him; changing our mortal bodies to be like His glorious body. Until we are caught up or carried out like Lazarus, we remain in this present world as a light to the lost sheep. We continue passing down the unaltered gospel, helping sheep hear the call and prepare themselves to enter the new kingdom.

Knowing and understanding that God speaks of more than one world in the Bible helps us grasp the mysteries of God's kingdom.

> *"For God so loved the world, that he gave his only begotten Son, that whosoever believeth in him should not perish, but have everlasting life." John 3:16*

The world in this scripture seems to refer to the entire human race. We will learn later in this chapter that the world is the field, and the field is purchased to claim the hidden treasure. This is what God did in John 3:16. He sent His son to become payment for the world (field) to get the treasure (church) hidden in the field. However, by revelation, we know that the world that Jesus speaks of is separate from those who are in and of the world because, those who are in and of the world are damned if they don't believe on Him:

> *"Even the Spirit of truth; whom the world cannot receive, because it seeth him not, neither knoweth him: but ye know him; for he dwelleth with you, and shall be in you." John 14:17*

"The world" that God loved so much that He gave His blood for, is the church. It is for everyone who obeys the divine call of God to be saved.

The church is the called out assembly of God (*ekklesia*). It is a body of believers who are conformed to the image that God predestined them to be; and they are faithful unto God and give Him glory in the earth (Romans 8:30, Revelation 17:14).

"But ye are a chosen generation, a royal priesthood, an holy nation, a peculiar people; that ye should shew forth the praises of him who hath called you out of darkness into his marvelous light." 1 Peter 2:9

The "peculiar people" Peter referred to, are a people spiritually called out from all other people in this present world. There are many other scriptures that show Christ's attention toward a particular people; and these people are worlds apart from others, separate from this present world, and hidden in Him before creation (predestined):

"And she shall bring forth a son, and thou shalt call his name JESUS: for he shall save his people from their sins." Matthew 1:21

Jesus will save His people! He will save a specific people that believe in Him, not all people.

"While I was with them in the world, I kept them in thy name: those that thou gavest me I have kept, and none of them is lost, but the son of perdition; that the scripture might be fulfilled." John 17:12

41

"I pray for them: I pray not for the world,
but for them which thou hast given me;
for they are thine." John 17:9

Again, Jesus is not anguishing in prayer over the entire world. Before He is led to be crucified, He is in the garden of Gethsemane travailing in prayer for people that have been "given" to Him.

"Even the Spirit of truth; whom the
world cannot receive, because it seeth
him not, neither knoweth him: but ye
know him; for he dwelleth with you, and
shall be in you." John 14:17

Now Jesus speaks of a relationship with those given to Him. How wonderful to know that a peaceful relationship with Jesus goes beyond this natural life – this present world.

"Behold, what manner of love the Father
hath bestowed upon us, that we should
be called the sons of God: therefore the
world knoweth us not, because it knew
him not." 1 John 3:1

Here the people are called sons of God, which further supports that there is a distinct relationship between a specific people and Jesus Christ.

"Yet a little while, and the world seeth me no more; but ye see me: because I live, ye shall live also." John 14:19

Everyone that strives to live Godly will suffer persecution. The suffering that God allows is not because God is a sadist. In fact, the Word is a record that there will be peace for those who endure hardship as good soldiers. The scriptures were written for our learning and edification so that we might rejoice while suffering in this present world. In the world ye shall have tribulation: but be of good cheer; I have overcome the world. (John 16:33).

There is another world that exists in the earth. It cannot be understood by things which we see with our natural eye, but it is seen when spiritually discerned or understood (1 Corinthians 2:7-14).

The church world has been called out of darkness in order to walk in light. Jesus could not have been speaking of the entire human race when He spoke of the world in John 3:16 because, those that are "of the world" live in darkness. Jesus further explains that the world loves darkness rather than light because their deeds are evil (John 3:18-21). When Jesus was being interrogated by Pilate, who inquired about Jesus being the king of the Jews, Jesus answered,

> *"...Thou sayest that I am a king. To this end was I born, and for this cause came I into the world, that I should bear witness unto the truth. Every one that is of the truth heareth my voice."*
> *John 18:37*

This scripture declares that there are a people who possess truth. And when the Christ of God speaks to these people, they hear Him and follow Him because they are of that truth. If the world hates the light, it hates truth. Jesus is truth, thus, a rejection of truth is a rejection of Jesus. This type of response to the glorious gospel of Jesus Christ is provoked by the spirit of the antichrist. Since we know that such a spirit cannot inherit the kingdom of God, it is evident that any creature existing by this spirit is not in the true church.

God called a people out from the world before the foundations of the world were laid. That is why Matthew recorded, "He shall save his people from their sins" (Acts 20:28). God prepared Himself a body and the blood of that body satisfied the righteous demands of a just God. This is the act of redemption, and not ownership. All souls belong to God who is the creator; however, only the redeemed body of believers have the privilege of being called sons of God. Many have literally heard the gospel while attending a physical church, but the testimony of God at the final judgment will declare whether or not they spiritually obeyed what they heard. God will make His final judgement of and testify whether or not He really knew people (Matthew 7:23).

Based on the writings of the Holy Spirit in the scriptures we call the Bible, I perceive that there have been two worlds and two natures of people operating in the earth throughout the dispensations. Until now, these two remain in the earth and grow together. Their relationship to God is like night and day.

CAIN AND ABEL

In the previous chapter, the nature of people in this present world are manifested to be in light or darkness. The record that God left for us concerning Cain and Abel gives a vivid illustration of people that possess these two opposing natures. These are the sons of Adam and Eve, the first recorded family of the earth. Inwardly, these sons were like night and day; and being brothers did not ease the animosity between them. Eventually, the tension that existed separated them.

These natures are representatives of what to expect from the families of the earth and their relationship with God.

> *"In this the children of God are manifest, and the children of the devil: whosoever doeth not righteousness is not of God, neither he that loveth not his brother."*
> *1 John 3:10*

Some lessons in the first book of John highlight brotherly kindness, obedience, faith in the Word of God, accountability, and rewards for actions. Saint John also used the scriptures concerning Cain and Abel to describe how the love of God was expressed, while showing the attitude of those who do not have God's love.

> *"Verily, verily, I say unto you, He that heareth my word, and believeth on him that sent me, hath everlasting life, and shall not come into condemnation; but is passed from death unto life." John 5:24*

> *"We know that we have passed from death unto life, because we love the brethren. He that loveth not his brother abideth in death." 1 John 3:14*

God is unchangeable and that makes His Word powerful and without end. Everything He spoke in the beginning of creation came to pass. We can see it unfold in the scriptures from Genesis to Revelation. An individual's regeneration is evidence of God's visible love for the body of Christ. That love that God imparts to His children must be manifested toward others, and is of no effect if it is expressed by lip service only.

Jesus commanded us to love, and His message is echoed in the epistles for the churches in the last days. According apostle John's writing, to if a person confesses allegiance to God, but hates his brother, he or she is deceived and walks in darkness. Reason, God is love; and to exhibit this dynamic character, believers must abide in His truth and His light.

If God's love demands we exist in light, then the children of darkness are incapable of expressing godly love (1 John 2:9). Their nature is to hate Christ and the children of light (Romans 1:30, 1 John 3:13-14). The church of God is challenged daily to let brotherly love continue, even amid the biting, devouring, and persecution of saints by false brethren (Matthew 5:44, 1 Peter 5:8). The consolation is in knowing we are being persecuted because of the light that shines in us. The world hates the children of light because these children represent Christ in the earth. Their sacrifices and good works testify that the works of the children of darkness are evil, which is why Cain slew Abel (John 7:7).

As a son of God, who was striving to be obedient to God, Abel was persecuted by his brother Cain. He was hated for his righteous deeds and his desire to please God. It was impossible for Cain to walk in light and darkness at the same time. He could not love Abel and hate him simultaneously. God is light, and in Him, there is no darkness at all. Therefore, mankind cannot have an equal distribution of light and darkness; one will eventually overcome the other.

Cain served God according to the ordinances given to him in his time, but his heart was far from God (Isaiah 29:13). Cain was a tiller of the ground and Abel was a keeper of sheep. God's response to Cain and Abel's sacrifice and offerings shows whether their heart was of the light or of darkness. While the Bible does not specifically indicate when and where Cain and Abel received their instructions for sacrificial service unto God, there are some revelatory indicators that they knew when to appear before God and what to bring (Genesis 4:3-6).

God ordained that peace and sin offerings be made with a blood sacrifice. As an example, He made atonement for the sin of Adam and Eve when He covered their nakedness (Genesis 3:21). The covering that God used was made of skin. Since Adam and Eve were the only type of their species at that time, the skin must have come from another creature of God that possessed blood.

We know clearly from God's response to Cain, that Cain's sacrifice was unacceptable because, his sacrifice was from the fruit of the ground. Abel's sacrifice pleased God because it demonstrated what God required for sin offerings. Abel offered God the firstling of his flock;

and he also gave of the fat, which belongs to God (Leviticus 3:16; 4:31; 16:25; 17:6).

Only blood could atone for sin and bring spiritual or eternal peace between God and man. Thus, Cain's sacrifice was ineffective. Abel voluntarily offered the fattest and choicest of his flock, which sent up a sweet-smelling savor unto the Lord. Cain became enraged at Abel, because Abel's offering magnified Cain's works, which fell short of God's requirements. His rebellious heart was exposed, proving he despised the chastisement and instruction of God. Cain thought the best from the ground was good enough to satisfy God. However, our best is never sufficient to please God. Being warned of his disobedience, Cain was overcome by a jealous and hateful spirit, which is the fruit of darkness; and this led to Cain killing his brother Abel.

Abel represents the called of God who present unto God a living, holy, and acceptable sacrifice (Romans 12:1). God testified Abel's sacrifice was righteous, empowering Abel's innocent blood to cry for vengeance from the grave. For, "By faith Abel offered unto God a more excellent sacrifice than Cain, by which he obtained witness that he was righteous, God testifying of his gifts: and by it he being dead yet speaketh" (Hebrews 11:4).

How was a dead man able to cry? The scriptures testify that the dead do not praise God. However, Abel was of the living — a child of the light. Abel's blood cried from out of the bosom of Abraham, a place of rest for the saints that died in faith (Luke 16:22).

The cry of Abel's blood was for vengeance. Abel was slain after he presented his sacrifice to God, and after he made atonement for sin and was declared righteous by God. Abel's blood spoke, however, the blood of the Lamb — which is Jesus Christ — speaks far better things than the blood of Abel. The blood of Christ atoned for the sins of the world and is for all those who believe and embrace His eternal sacrifice by faith. It is for the true church: a people called by God who follow him into everlasting life (Daniel 12:2, John 3:36).

Cain represents the false church, or those who offer unacceptable worship to God. In the time of Cain and Abel, the sacrifice was animals, but now man must present themselves freely through the sanctified blood of Jesus Christ (Ephesians 2:13, Colossians 1:20). Our sacrifice must be in spirit and in truth, and not like Cain, who used worldly logic and as a result, stumbled at the truth.

Mankind was created to give praise to God and reflect His glory – this is true worship. Because man was in sin, he could not genuinely praise God, man's sins had to be covered. Cain was spiritually dead while he lived, and made him unable to truly praise God. The dead praise not the LORD, neither any that go down into silence (Psalm 115:17).

God used the testimony of Abel as evidence that those who are in Christ live forever. Abel did not go silently to the grave, his blood was speaking because he had the light of life (John 8:12). Had Cain been a child of the light, he would have repented of his sin and offered a more perfect sacrifice to invoke peace between him and God. His actions proved he was a child of darkness, and he was cast out of the presence of God, and lived in a state of condemnation.

It was after the death of Abel and the birth of Seth's son Enos that men began to worship God. Cain's crime showed more clearly the impact that Adam's transgression had on the world. In the midst of this chaotic situation, God would not leave Himself without a witness in the earth. After Eve bore Seth, men began to call on the Lord. While the earth was being populated with many sons wickedness increased, until the appointed time when God manifested Himself to the children of promise.

Part II Parables of the Two

"Judas saith unto him, not Iscariot, Lord, how is it that thou wilt manifest thyself unto us, and not unto the world?" John 14:2

THE LOST COIN

"Either what woman having ten pieces of silver, if she lose one piece, doth not light a candle, and sweep the house, and seek diligently till she find it?" Luke 15:8

"And when she hath found it, she calleth her friends and her neighbours together, saying, Rejoice with me; for I have found the piece which I had lost." Luke 15:9

This parable is part of a group of parables that describes God's love for His church. Jesus likens God unto a woman who searches for a lost coin. This coin is part of a set of ten silver pieces that she possesses. Just as the woman searched for her lost coin, God spoke light into darkness to assist Him in recovering all that were lost in the world.

Students of the Bible should note that what was lost in the house belonged to the woman. This gives us a better understanding of redemption. We can see how God formulated a plan to recapture those who are a part of the church but are lost in the world through the sin of Adam.

The woman knew where the coin was. The coin

was in the house. The woman did not search for all types of coins that could possibly be in the house. This woman searched for a specific coin, which was part of the ten that belonged to her. Likewise, God searches for His people, not all people but a specific people. God encountered one of His sons while being crucified. One of His children spoke to Jesus while they both were hanging on crucifixes. He said unto Jesus, "Lord, remember me when thou comest into thy kingdom" (Luke 23:42). This man was on the cross was one of two malefactors that hung on either side of Jesus. These two malefactors were in the same sin condition and were condemned to die as punishment for their crimes. However, one was in the mind of Christ while He was hanging, sacrifice His life to save His people. One thief was condemned to eternal death, and the other thief was welcomed into the kingdom of God by the mediator between God and man, Jesus (Luke 23:43).

Just like God searches for members of the church until He completes it, the woman relentlessly sought the lost coin. She never doubted that the coin was within her reach as she lit a candle to begin the search in her house (Luke 15:8). God never loses count of those who belong to Him. He knew how, why, and what it would take to recover all of His children who were separated from Him. Whenever God finds one of His children, that child receives the Holy Ghost and cries, "Abba Father;" thus, testifying that God is their father. The Spirit of God seals them, and they are marked for eternal life. Like that coin was found in the woman's house in the parable, everyone in the church is found and identified by the Holy Spirit that searches the field.

THE HIDDEN TREASURE

"Again, the kingdom of heaven is like unto treasure hid in a field; the which when a man hath found, he hideth, and for joy thereof goeth and selleth all that he hath, and buyeth that field."
Matthew 13:44

Another parable used to describe the church world in the kingdom of God is Jesus' illustration of hidden treasure in a field. The blood of God was and is the atonement for mankind. It is powerful enough to redeem all that will believe on Him. With this thought, what was hidden in the field must be the church. After the Spirit of God diligently searched and identified the treasure, that treasure was hidden in Christ. And for the joy of that precious jewel, the Son of God offered up His body. The Son's bloody sacrifice was the payment, and with that blood He purchased the entire world. He had to gain possession of the entire world to regain legal ownership of the treasure that was hidden in it. This is a description of John 3:16. God loves the church (those hidden in the field) so much the He purchased the world with His own blood. For example, when someone loses their home to foreclosure, they lose everything that is left in the house. The person or company that buys the house, purchases the home with its contents. If the original owners want any contents the left in the home, they must be able to purchase the house to collect any contents they deem to be of value.

The church is hidden in the world, and exists in the heavenly kingdom of God. It is the place where God is adored, where angels ascend and descend, and where the saints have access to God. Jesus told His disciples to pray for this kingdom to rule in the earth (Matthew 6:10). His kingdom was an everlasting kingdom, unlike the realm of this world that will soon pass away (Matthew 4:8).

> *"For the kingdom of God is not meat and drink; but righteousness, and peace, and joy in the Holy Ghost." Romans 14:17*

The kingdom of God is not an earthly kingdom, it is a spiritual kingdom. In it, the saints are spiritually preserved, while yet remaining in the earth (Luke 17:21, 1 Corinthians 4:20). In this kingdom we call, "the world," Jesus said we will have tribulation. The trouble comes from being born into the world and from Satan, who is the ruler of this world. Both believer and non-believer experience trouble in this world. Nevertheless, there is comfort in the Holy Ghost because in Christ's kingdom, we shall have peace (John 16:33).

There are documented incidents of the operation of God's kingdom on the earth. In the Old Testament, Jacob left home after receiving his brother Esau's birthright. He stopped in Luz while on his way to his Uncle Laban's house. While sleeping on the ground with a rock for a pillow, Jacob saw the kingdom of God.

> *"And he dreamed, and behold a ladder set up on the earth, and the top of it reached to heaven: and behold the angels of God ascending and descending on it." Genesis 28:12*

It was in this place that God assured Jacob that He would be with him. It was also here that God told Jacob that He would keep him everywhere he went, and would bring him back to his home.

> *"And Jacob awaked out of his sleep, and he said, Surely the LORD is in this place; and I knew it not." Genesis 28:16*

The kingdom of God was and is in the world, though this world is filled with the threat of war and death. It is so comforting to know that we have access to God while in the middle of our troubles, and amid the chaotic conditions of this world. Not only did Jacob grow in his awareness of the presence of God, but he also testified that God's glory was in the earth. God left this testimony on record to encourage every believer that He will bring to pass everything He promised. Every believer can rejoice in this testimony because Jacob returned to his homeland in peace as God promised.

All regenerated man can see God's glory in the earth through Christ Jesus, which is the only access whereby man can see, understand, or live in God's presence.

> *"And he saith unto him, Verily, verily, I say unto you, Hereafter ye shall see heaven open, and the angels of God ascending and descending upon the Son of man." John 1:51*

Another witness of the power of God in the earth is Old Testament scriptures about a Syrian king who sought an opportunity to defeat Israel. God exposed the king's plan to Elisha the prophet in order to save Israel. When the King of Syria found out that the man of God was revealing his strategy, he sent a host of soldiers to capture Elisha. As the Syrian host surrounded the city, Elisha's servant became fearful and wondered how they would escape such a great army. Elisha said, "Fear not, they that be with us are more than they that be with them" (2 Kings 6:16). This powerful statement was revelatory for both the servant and those who read about the God of Israel. No matter how overwhelming the threats are from the enemy, God is more than everyone who is against the children of God.

Elisha's words were consistent with the truth of God's kingdom as illustrated throughout the Bible.

> *"Though an host should encamp against me, my heart shall not fear: though war should rise against me, in this will I be confident." Psalm 27:3*

Having knowledge of the kingdom of God not only comforts the hearts of believers, but it also gives saints an assurance that God is with us in trouble and spiritual warfare. Though the battle seems great, God has given the church a sure hope: we have and will overcome.

> *"Ye are of God, little children, and have overcome them: because greater is he that is in you, than he that is in the world." 1 John 4:4*

Elisha's servant did not see God's army until God opened his eyes. The light of God reveals things the things of God, as well as things done in darkness.

God hid his purchased possession, the church, in a world of unbelievers. Because His domain is not of this world, this reality is not clearly understood by the carnally minded. For example, Jesus told a Jewish ruler named Nicodemus who feared to approach him by day, "Verily, verily, I say unto thee, except a man be born again, he cannot see the kingdom of God" (John 3:3).

The world that we live in and God's world are worlds apart. To enter either of the worlds, a person must be born into them. The natural-born man can grasp and perceive natural things, but in order to understand and enter into God's world or kingdom, that man must be born again.

> *"Not every one that saith unto me, Lord, Lord, shall enter into the kingdom of heaven; but he that doeth the will of my Father which is in heaven." Matthew 7:21*

By His own blood, God redeemed the souls of those who were lost in Adam and hid them in the church of

Jesus Christ. However, there is another redemption to come. The final redemption is to glorify the bodies of the saints. This great salvation also includes the changing of our mortal, or earthly bodies. When we were called by the gospel, it was to be saved from sin. When we were selected, we were to be sanctified unto God. And when the Lord comes for us, we will be changed to be received in the heavens with the Bridegroom (1 Corinthians 15:51-54). This is the hope of all the children of God.

The church is waiting for the redeeming of our bodies from corruption to glorification. We will have a body that never dies and is eternal in the heavens; and again, this is earnest of our inheritance until the redemption of the purchased possession unto the praise of his glory (Ephesians 1:14, Romans 8:23, 1 Corinthians 15:49, Philippians 3:21, 1 Peter 1:4)

THE PEARL OF GREAT PRICE

"Again, the kingdom of heaven is like unto a merchant man, seeking goodly pearls." Matthew 13:45

"Who, when he had found one pearl of great price, went and sold all that he had, and bought it." Matthew 13:46

Along with a group of parables describing the heavenly kingdom, Jesus likens the kingdom of heaven to that of a buyer seeking goodly pearls. In this parable, the merchant man is looking for goodly pearls, which suggests he appreciates and has knowledge about the object he seeks. This merchant man can pinpoint special characteristics of the jewels he seeks and determine its value. He is like a curator or art collector who studies and then prepares a resting place to house the objects after it is found or purchased.

Like the merchant man, the spirit of the living God scours the earth until He finds His jewel, and a great price is paid to secure it. Note that in the Bible, the merchant man sought pearls, plural, yet he surrendered all that he had to purchase one pearl of great value. Likewise, God commendeth His love toward us, in that, while we were yet sinners, plural, Christ died for the church, singular (Romans 5:8). Like the man who purchased the field for the hidden treasure, God purchased the one pearl from among many pearls. He did this by His own blood, which is the blood of Jesus Christ. It was a magnificent price to pay, but like the merchant man, His choice was not due to our value alone, but it is because of God's desire and love for the object that He seeks.

It is not a mystery that God loves us and prepared a sacrifice for the atonement of our sins. His love and preparation are for the jewel He sought, and that love is not based on appearance. The treasure is beneath the surface – it's on how God imagined it should be. The price that was paid on Golgotha's Hill was for the world in order to obtain the hidden jewel.

> *"For many are called, but few are chosen." Matthew 22:14*

There was only one pearl that God procured with the blood of His Son, and that pearl is the church. He drew them by His love and preserves them in Christ Jesus.

> *"Jude, the servant of Jesus Christ, and brother of James, to them that*

are sanctified by God the Father, and
preserved in Jesus Christ, and called:
Mercy unto you, and peace, and love,
be multiplied." Jude 1:1-2

This pearl will not perish with the wood and stubble of the world because God has power to preserve it. Like a curator keeps his possessions, those whom God has called and chosen are born again into Jesus Christ, and the body and the spirit are kept until the coming of the Lord.

"Neither do men put new wine into old
bottles: else the bottles break, and the
wine runneth out, and the bottles perish:
but they put new wine into new bottles,
and both are preserved." Matthew 9:17

God preserves His jewel through regeneration. In regeneration, or being born again, His children are become new through the washing of their entire bodies in water (baptized), and then the body being filled with the Spirit of Christ (new wine).

Remembering that in the scripture, "Both are preserved," our bodies must be washed and filled with the Spirit of Christ. We cannot be preserved until the Lord comes if the process is incomplete. A person with only the baptism in water is an empty vessel. And if a body displays signs of the spirit without having been baptized in water, at the time of resurrection, the spirit will go back to God and the body will be burned.

> *"But ye are not in the flesh, but in the Spirit, if so be that the Spirit of God dwell in you. Now if any man have not the Spirit of Christ, he is none of his."*
> *Romans 8:9*

The eternal Spirit of God saves and keeps both the regenerated body and soul until the body is changed to the image of Christ.

> *"And the very God of peace sanctify you wholly; and I pray God your whole spirit and soul and body be preserved blameless unto the coming of our Lord Jesus Christ." 1 Thessalonians 5:23*

The pearl, or church, is hidden in Christ because He is the transforming power of God. When Jesus rose from the dead, He received all power in heaven and in earth. Having this authority gave Him the right to redeem us from sin. Since He is the only man who died and rose again, He is able to give life to all those that believe in His name.

Like the merchant man, God found goodly pearls and called us out from all the other pearls in the sea. When He called us, we were lost in sin; and being dead in sin, we could not save ourselves. We could not pay price required for the ransom. Only God, the merchant man, could delivered us, and He did. He saved us! We are that pearl of great price! is A righteous conglomerate of crystals that make up the jewel; shaped, nourished, and hidden in the earth by the good seed: Jesus Christ.

THE GOOD SEED

> *"Another parable put he forth unto them, saying, The kingdom of heaven is likened unto a man which sowed good seed in his field." Matthew 13:24*

This is one of the most popular parables because teachers can relate to the natural terms Jesus used. In this parable, the field is the world, the children of God are the wheat, and the children of the devil are the tares. In a careful analysis of these verses, you will see a clear picture of the kingdom of God as it operates in the earth and the manifestation of the good seed.

God had a recovery plan for all His see that were lost after the fall of man. When God cursed the serpent for his deception in the garden, He promised that there would be conflict between His seed and the seed of the serpent. He also said the seed of the woman would triumph over the serpent's offspring (Genesis 3:15); "And the dragon was wroth with the woman, and went to make war with the remnant of her seed, which keep the commandments of God, and have the testimony of Jesus Christ" (Revelation 12:17). The seed of the woman is Jesus Christ, and the woman is Israel, which the apostle Paul calls the, "Church in the wilderness."

According to this prophecy, Israel would be persecuted by the enemy until he is defeated by Christ.

It did look hopeless for the world after Adam sinned. Since that fall, Satan has been deceiving many from generation to generation. To this day, his seed continues to make war with the woman Israel. However, neither Satan, nor his seed would deceive the earth forever, as prophesied God would raise up another seed unto Himself. This new seed would not be born the consummation of man or artificial means. This seed came through many generations beginning with Abraham, and it was born of a virgin.

God is not like man when it comes to promises. God is faithful. He made a promise in Adam's day concerning the birth of an overcoming seed and reaffirmed it through the fathers and the prophets; and it was confirmed in Jesus Christ. Isaiah prophesied that a branch would grow out of the roots of Jesse, the father of David, and Jesus declared in the book of Revelations that He was that root (Isaiah 11:10, Revelation 22:16).

Jesus is the seed that will bring peace to the children of Israel. His kingdom would be an everlasting kingdom, and He would govern Israel perpetually.

*"Now to Abraham and his seed were
the promises made. He saith not, And
to seeds, as of many; but as of one,
And to thy seed, which is Christ."
Galatians 3:16*

The promises pertaining Christ's government was made to Abraham, and then to the children of promise. God made Abraham a father of many nations according to the flesh, that He might produce spiritual offspring of faith. Like Israel, this seed would be a remnant in the earth. This promised seed was composed of the natural seed of Abraham and they that are born of the faith of Jesus Christ, they are counted as the seed (Galatians 3:29, Romans 4:16).

The mystery of the kingdom of God is this: God wanted men that would reflect His glory as a glass of crystal reflects the glow of the sunlight. This was the purpose of the creation of man, to bear the image and likeness of God.

Satan was banished from heaven and from his position next to God. He was removed as the morning star because he was spoiled with pride, and refused to reflect the glory of God (Ezekiel 28:13-17, Revelation 12:13, Isaiah 14:12). His lust for self-promotion changed his existence into darkness, and he could no longer reflect the light and glory of his Creator. In order for an object to cast an image, light must be present. Lucifer had no light because his desires were sinful. His sin put him on an unchangeable path. A path of no return. Because he had works of darkness, it separated him from the glory of God, which is the light.

God planted His seed in the earth to bring forth fruit in His image and after His likeness. He wanted goodly children, so He planted good seed, which is Jesus the Christ (the Word made flesh). This seed would produce much fruit but not without a great price.

> *"Verily, verily, I say unto you, Except a corn of wheat fall into the ground and die, it abideth alone: but if it die, it bringeth forth much fruit." John 12:24*

Jesus had to die in the earth and be resurrected in order to reproduce others like Him. If a seed is not planted in the earth, it will just be a seed by itself. However, if you put a seed in the ground and nurture it, the seed will grow and bring forth more seed as itself. The church is the fruit of Jesus Christ, and the plants that the servants did not plant, are tares planted by that wicked one, Satan.

WHEAT AND TARES

"But while men slept, his enemy came and sowed tares among the wheat, and went his way." Matthew 13:25

To have an abundant church, God planted good seed in the earth. As with any planting, a farmer must tend to his crop for it to yield a favorable harvest. So, God set watchmen over the field just as He set Adam over Eden. In this parable, God planted good seed, so it would undoubtedly return good fruit. But while the watchmen slept, Satan planted bad seed among the grain of wheat. These were not wheat, could not become wheat, and were much more than weeds. These were wicked plantings.

Watchmen are the tillers who nourish and care for the sheep, and warn them when the wolf is coming. For thus hath the Lord said unto me, "Go, set a watchman, let him declare what he seeth" (Isaiah 21:6). Unfortunately, there are times when the watchmen shirk their responsibility.

"His watchmen are blind: they are all ignorant, they are all dumb dogs, they

cannot bark; sleeping, lying down, loving to slumber." Isaiah 56:10

As Adam and Eve did in the garden, some of these watchmen are blinded by their lust, and ultimately, they fail the position for which they are called.

While some slept or were not watchful, the enemy of God took advantage of the breach and planted false seed in the earth.

"But when the blade was sprung up, and brought forth fruit, then appeared the tares also." Matthew 13:26

About now you may be questioning whether this is true. Aren't all the people in the world children of God? Did it really happen like this? Yes. It did happen. No, all people in the earth are not the children of God. Some were planted by God's enemy. These tares were the offspring of Satan and had the form of wheat because they grew with the wheat. The laborers recognized the tares because unlike the wheat, they yielded no fruit. For every tree is known by its own fruit.

"So the servants of the householder came and said unto him, Sir, didst not

*thou sow good seed in thy field? from
whence then hath it tares?" Matthew
13:27*

After the ministers (servants) recognized that
certain seeds were taking on another form after they
matured, they went to God (householder). The ministers
made inquiry of how tares could be in God's field, since
God had planted wheat only. He said unto them, "An
enemy hath done this." Then the servants asked God if
He wanted them to gather up the tares from among the
wheat (Matthew 13:28). "But he said, Nay; lest while
ye gather up the tares, ye root up also the wheat with
them" (Matthew 13:29).

So then, in the world, there are sons of God and
there are sons of the enemy of God — both grow side
by side until the time of eternal separation. God will
not allow His servants to pull up the tares because in
the process of pulling up the tares some of the wheat
may be removed prematurely. This can happen when
the wheat is pulled up during a stage when both the
wheat and tares resemble each other or have similar
characteristics. The Lord is not like man, He looks,
"Not as man seeth; for man looketh on the outward
appearance, but the Lord looketh on the heart" (1
Samuel 16:7).

The ministers in this parable knew the difference between the wheat and the tares because they knew God and the nature of the good seed. The good seed is Jesus Christ; and His fruit and His seed mature to resemble Him. However, the tares were not like the wheat. Nothing tares do could earn them the right to be called the planting of the Lord because they originated from the wicked one – seed of the wicked one.

God works according to His schedule. At the appointed time, He will judge the earth for sin, and He will have the tares plucked up by the root. Our God will come and avenge the elect who are persecuted by Satan's seed. Yes! Jesus will come again and render judgment on the tares of this world, as well as the enemy that planted them. Although the longsuffering of God provides time for the enemy to work evil, those who work evil will not go unpunished. Every plant which our heavenly Father has not planted, shall be rooted up at the end of the world (Matthew 15:13).

As prophesied, there was and is great enmity between the good seed and the seed of the devil. Since the beginning of his fall from heaven, Satan purposed to gain the attention of the universe. He petitioned the assistance of a third of the angels in heaven to join him in overthrowing the throne of God. Since he failed in this effort, he seeks to destroy the glory of God, which is man.

Satan's greatest satisfaction is in killing the saints or provoking them to destroy others, bite or devour each other, or curse God. Satan's main objective is to destroy the last Adam that would redeem the righteous seed who were lost in the first Adam.

When the dragon saw that he was cast unto the earth, he persecuted the woman which brought forth the man child (Revelation 12:13). As previously stated, the woman that brought forth the man-child is Israel: the church in the wilderness. The man-child is the seed: Jesus Christ. This is the man-child that Satan worked through King Herod to kill (Matthew 2:13). Herod feared losing his advantage in his earthly kingdom at the coming of the prophesied Messiah, so he had many children slain. It didn't work! He didn't find Jesus because that Holy Thing was hidden in Egypt.

God allows Satan a short time on the earth for His use and purposes. The wicked one roams the earth trying to steal, kill, and destroy God's creation (John 10:10). He steals truth from those who lack understanding of the word of God. He kills those he is permitted to, and he tries to destroy the influence and the souls of the righteous (Mark 4:15, James 5:6, Luke 6:22).

John the Baptist lauds the good seed and announces the coming of His kingdom with power and judgment. His cry of repentance prepares the bride for her Groom, and those who repent are adorned and make themselves ready by separating themselves from their ungodly nature.

The Word is a purifier, discerner of thoughts and evil intents, and a separator of the wheat and the tares (Matthew 3:12). The good seed are sanctified by the Word of God, and the evidence of the seed falling on good ground is seen in their response to the gospel.

THE TEN VIRGINS

"Then shall the kingdom of heaven be likened unto ten virgins, which took their lamps, and went forth to meet the bridegroom." Matthew 25:1

The term virgin naturally refers to a person, who outside of the affection from their family, has never experienced any physical relations with another in consummation of their union. In this parable, Christ reveals the true evidence of those in the Bride. The virgins here refer to those who have heard the report of the Bridegroom (as Rebecca heard about Isaac) and embark on a journey to meet Him for the purpose of marriage. They remain chaste and devoted to their Bridegroom until his appearing. Like virgins of old, these ladies in waiting go through a process of sanctification and purification in complete anticipation and preparation to meet their bridegroom. Those who are chosen will be presented to Christ as a chaste virgin.

The hope of the virgins is to be joined with the bridegroom; and that is what strengthens their patience. In that the exact time of His appearance is unknown, the virgins must remain in a state of readiness so that when they are summoned, they are fully prepared to leave, and have power to make the journey.

From the words of Christ regarding the end of the world, we can see that there are 'two women' or 'two churches' in the earth. Every dispensation has had, and will have, false religious systems until the end of the world. The one system God recognizes is based on election and His plan of salvation, which He drafted before the world was created. The other system is powered by the devil and will work until it is completely destroyed by the coming of Christ with the saints. During the time of great tribulation, a remnant will worship the true and living God. These will be persecuted by the false church or the great whore Babylon that sitteth upon many waters and reigneth over the kings of the earth (Revelation 17:1, 18).

The two types of women or the ten virgins in the earth are like the wheat and the tares, which grow up together; and like the wheat and tares their works confirm their eternal end, and ultimately God's reapers will separate them from those that were chosen to enter the bridal chamber.

The kingdom of God has regenerated virgins, which are called and chosen of God. However, the false virgins are among the called, but are not chosen of God unto salvation. They walk, live, or work with the righteous, but only have a form of godliness; and ignorantly reject the everlasting gospel of Christ (Revelation 14:6).

The ten virgins prepare to meet the bridegroom who they heard about through the messenger of Jesus Christ. Five are wise and five are foolish. The virgins wisdom, or lack therefore, have nothing to do with earthly customs or traditions. The wisdom that is at work in this parable is of God — spiritual wisdom or foolishness.

Many are called to the wedding, but few are chosen, as in the days of King Ahasuerus, when he searched for a bride. Jesus' reference to five of the ten as foolish directly relates to their faith and obedience to what they have heard regarding the bridegroom; and hidden in the details of what they heard, is the knowledge of what they needed to meet Him. Jesus said, "And every one that heareth these sayings of mine, and doeth them not, shall be likened unto a foolish man, which built his house upon the sand" (Matthew 7:26). The foolish virgins worked, but their works were in vain because, they were not what the bridegroom required. God is the architect of His house and our salvation. If a man's works are not according to His specifications, what a man produces will be inadequate and will not reflect God's glory.

The foolish women heard the gospel but did not obey the gospel. Professing themselves to be wise, they became fools (Romans 1:22). The foolish virgins were like people warming themselves by the fire (power of the Holy Spirit), but never having the fire dwelling in them. Just as John the Baptist told people how to prepare to receive Jesus through repentance, how to be ready for the Bridegroom was revealed to the virgins. What they heard was truth; and their obedience was evidence that they believed what they heard; and proof they had faith in the Bridegroom's return.

The spirit and the knowledge of God enlightened the five wise virgins on how to worship and dwell in the kingdom of God; and the other five had their understanding darkened by the enemy, and they ultimately stumbled at the word or commandments, having not the truth.

> *"Are there not twelve hours in the day?*
> *If any man walk in the day, he stumbleth*
> *not, because he seeth the light of this*
> *world. But if a man walk in the night, he*

stumbleth, because there is no light in him." John 11:9-10

The words of Christ and how to please the Bridegroom is by the revelation from God. When Peter confessed that Jesus was the Christ, Jesus let him know that this kind of knowledge came from God and not man. God must unveil His will and purpose to man in order for man to have the ability to see, understand, know, and do His will. We cannot clearly see the things of God without His revelation.

> *"The secret things belong unto the LORD our God: but those things which are revealed belong unto us and to our children for ever, that we may do all the words of this law." Deuteronomy 29:29*

Some may believe that revelation is not required to obey God; and that individuals can just read or study the scriptures and understand what God wants from man. However, this parable proves that revelation from God is required to know His will. Until God opens our eyes to His secrets, we can read or see naturally, without having any depth or spiritual understanding.

On their journey to meet the bridegroom, the

foolish virgins took their lamps, but took no oil. The wise virgins took oil in their vessels with their lamps. It is important to note that the wise virgins had a vessel with them for the oil. Saint Matthew is the only recorder of this parable. There are no supporting scriptures to corroborate that the foolish virgins had vessels of oil with their lamps. However, we know that they didn't take what was necessary because Christ calls them foolish.

It is evident that all ten virgins started on the journey, however, they did not all have the same destination. So, what the wise virgins felt was required to finish the journey, was seemingly not necessary to the foolish. Why is this important? The virgins ability to obey directions, was based on their knowledge and understanding of how to meet the Bridegroom. The question may be asked, "If all of the virgins were called and chosen to be the bride of Christ, shouldn't they all be carrying the same things needed for their journey?" Yes. Everyone who is called and chosen of God unto salvation is given knowledge, understanding, and a measure of the faith to do what God purposed to obtain eternal salvation.

> *"Having made known unto us the mystery of his will, according to his*

*good pleasure which he hath purposed
in himself." Ephesians 1:9*

*"For it is God which worketh in you both
to will and to do of his good pleasure."
Philippians 2:13*

If God calls someone for a specific purpose, He
will equip that person to perform the task. For example,
when building the tabernacle, God called Bezaleel of
the tribe of Judah by name, and told Moses, "... I have
filled him with the spirit of God, in wisdom, and in
understanding, and in knowledge, and in all manner of
workmanship" (Exodus 31:3). Also, when Solomon was
chosen by God to build Him a house, he said:

> *"Only the Lord give thee wisdom and
> understanding, and give thee charge
> concerning Israel, that thou mayest,
> keep the law of the Lord thy God." 1
> Chronicles. 22:12*

When God reveals his purpose for an individual's
existence, He will also give that person the knowledge
and ability to fulfill that purpose. God is the one who
imparts wisdom, knowledge, and understanding of how

to walk according to His will, and that is also done despite the present state of an individual.

From a natural perspective, the ten virgins lived in the same condition. However, inwardly they walked according to the knowledge they had received from God. The ten virgins were spiritually separated by their knowledge of what pleases God. How is that possible? God speaks to the spirit of man and shows man how to delight in Him, as well as how man can become His delight. This includes the time when man is ignorant of God. God discloses Himself at His own will; and at the appointed time His secrets are revealed.

All ten of the virgins heard the gospel and were called to the marriage. Each set of virgins had lamps, but not all were clothed in the required wedding garments; not all had been justified and would be glorified. How do we know this? Only five virgins were chosen (many called, few chosen). These five had wisdom from God. They had a 'known' relationship with God, where God knows the individual and the individual knows God. God showed us the 'known' relationship that the Bridegroom has with the five virgins, look at Adam and Eve. When Adam 'knew' Eve, she conceived a child. To conceive a child that means they consummated their union – or went into the bridal chamber. If there is no consummation, God will not 'know' you.

The lamps that the virgins carried were to light their way through the dark and give direction, and all of the virgins had lamps. However, as with any lamp, despite the measure of oil when you first use it, lamps can run out. As a result, wicks burn out, leaving the carrier in the dark. The five wise virgins received wisdom from God to keep oil in their lamps and in another vessel; a planned overflow, if you will. The knowledge God gave to half of the virgins would give them life, and the little knowledge of God obtained by the foolish would soon burn out.

> *"The light of the righteous rejoiceth: but*
> *the lamp of the wicked shall be put out."*
> *Proverbs 13:9*

After David was delivered from the hands of King Saul, he praised God and sang, "For thou art my lamp, O Lord: and the Lord will lighten my darkness" (2 Samuel 22:29). In the manner of David, the virgins were called out of darkness and had the light of God to brighten the course of their lives. After entering the bridal chamber with the Bridegroom, these virgins will rejoice and eternally sing praises of deliverance as David.

All ten virgins slumbered and slept until the cry was made to go out to meet the Bridegroom. When they heard the cry, "Then all those virgins arose, and trimmed their lamps" (Matthew 25:7). To enter in with the bridegroom, all of the virgins had to trim their lamps. This would allow the lamp to shine brighter. However, trimming alone would not be enough. Trimming is like the putting away the filth of the flesh – which has never been enough. Trimming helps the lamp shine brighter, but the oil that fuels the lamp is what makes it shine.

The wise had another vessel with oil. This typifies a born-again believer who has been baptized in the name of Jesus and filled with the Holy Ghost. Jesus said you can't put new wine in old bottles. All ten virgins represent old bottles, which is why they had to trim. But the other vessel that the wise had was Jesus Christ, which they put on in baptism.

While getting ready to go forth to meet the bridegroom, the foolish confessed that their lamps had burned out and they had no oil. They were like many people who started out with the church, but in the day of trouble they fainted. Many are not able to make the journey because they have a surface relationship with God – not a 'known' relationship. The five foolish virgins looked to the wise to give them some oil; to share enough with the foolish so they could make the journey.

The foolish realized they needed light, but had no oil to fuel the lamp. The future looked surprisingly dim for the five foolish, because the wise virgins would not share their oil. The wise encouraged the foolish virgins to go to their previous suppliers and purchase their oil, or rather go to them that buy and sell. From a natural point of view this response may make the wise virgins seem callous and void of compassion, seeing they had oil in another vessel. Sharing would have been a logical decision in such a desperate time, and then all of the virgins might have had the ability to make the journey. But we must remember that this is a revelation of spiritual things. These virgins were preparing to meet Jesus and were told to be ready. There is not enough time to work when night comes and the cry is made (Matthew 9:4), and there is no option of sharing the Spirit of God, which is a type of seal from God that an individual belongs to the family of God; and if it is a seal of a 'known' relationship, God would we be the one to supply that need.

The wise could not give the foolish virgins power to become sons of God, nor the privilege to be in the bride, that is a work of Christ. This parable reveals that there is an eternal relationship between Christ and the church, which will be celebrated by the marriage of the Lamb. Many were invited, but few are chosen. The chosen are adorned with salvation, which is the wedding garment of the Lamb's wife. All that have made themselves ready are given entrance into the bridal or bedchamber. And "afterward came also the other virgins, saying, Lord, Lord, open to us" (Matthew 25:11).

The unwise virgins crying after the bridegroom, pleading with Him to open the chamber door is an animated reflection of the earth during the flood. Though Noah preached the gospel and warned people to come into the ark because it was going to rain, like the foolish virgins, many were disobedient; and they were ill-prepared for the journey and therefore did not escape. They were shut out of the ark when the earth was flooded. Can you imagine people trying to get into the ark when the waters rose to unimaginable heights? Like Noah, the church receives enough grace for life, and they receive wisdom for the journey; and all these blessings are given from God to escape the wrath to come.

Although the wrath of God is waiting to come on the world, there is good news! There is a way of escape and that way is through the gospel of Jesus Christ.

Though the gospel compels man to put on Christ through baptism, many will not hear, and that will leave them without the necessary garments to enter into the paradise of God. The ark and the garment are the same. They are a covering and a hiding place from the storm to come. All of those that are in the bride of Christ have that covering.

The bride is the children of God who are redeemed from among the world and are kept by the power of God; not because of anything they have done, but because they have been called, chosen, and sanctified to glorify God in the earth. Their consolation or reward for obedience is to meet their Lord face to face.

In this parable of the virgins, the wise remained chaste unto the coming of the Lord and were unmoved by the doctrine of Jezebel and the whoredom of Babylon the great, mother of harlots (Revelation 2:18-26, 17:1-6) whose purpose is to deceive the bride and cause her to fail on the journey.

> *"These are they which were not defiled with women; for they are virgins. These are they which follow the Lamb whithersoever he goeth. These were redeemed from among men, being the*

firstfruits unto God and to the Lamb."
Revelation 14:4

Out of all the nations in the earth God chose Israel to worship Him. Before the flood there were sons of God and sons of men, and the same is true after the flood. God will have a people for His namesake regardless of the wickedness of men and the increasingly evil days. As there was a remnant during the flood, there is a remnant redeemed from among men today, and they are one nation under God.

Part III Two Nations

"And the LORD said unto her, Two nations are in thy womb, and two manner of people shall be separated from thy bowels." Genesis 25:2

Esau And Jacob

"And the LORD said unto her, two nations are in thy womb, and two manner of people shall be separated from thy bowels; and the one people shall be stronger than the other people; and the elder shall serve the younger."
Genesis 25:23

God consistently reveals throughout the Bible who His children are, as well as their trials and triumphs in every dispensation. Some of the simplest analogies used, show His divine intentions toward His people. Types like Cain and Abel, Esau and Jacob, and Isaac and Ishmael.

Cain and Abel were the first brothers recorded in the Bible. Their history was written for us to remember the effects of sin on the earth's family; and to understand God's relationship and dealings with believers and unbelievers.

The second notable duo was Esau and Jacob. It is clearly not a coincidence that in each of these relationships, the unbeliever was the elder brother. God's will defies the customs and standards of this world therefore, God ordained that the elder serve the younger. This is a type of Adam (flesh) serving Christ (Spirit). This principal was made evident by God empowering Jacob to grab Esau's heel in the womb.

Traditionally, the elder brother would be first in line to receive inheritance and blessings from his father, and he had the first right of redemption of land and property from debtors in every case. However, God ordained that in cases where the elder brother or next of kin rejects his birthright or refuses his right to redeem, the elder is then subservient to the younger brother. This was commonplace in Israel, and it is so in the kingdom of God. Although he was the elder brother, Esau had to serve Jacob. This reversal was due to Esau's rejection of his birthright, or rights of firstborn (Hebrews 12:16).

In the times of Jacob and Esau, it was customary for a father to call the children to receive their blessing and inheritance before he died. In that the elder brother was usually first, he would receive the greater portion of the inheritance.

Along with a prophetic synopsis of each son's identity and posterity among the people, Israel (Jacob) called his sons in their order and by faith, began to bless them. Joseph being fully aware of the process was displeased when his father Israel laid his right hand upon Ephraim's head for blessing. He knew that Manasseh was the elder and should receive the greater blessing. However, Israel (Jacob) knew that Ephraim would become many nations and be greater than his elder brother Manasseh; therefore, Israel refused Joseph's plea to let the brothers switch places, and proceeded to bless Ephraim first (Genesis 48:17-19).

Also, in a lesson of God's sovereignty and grace, Paul teaches us that all Israel is not Israel (Romans 9:6); meaning, many may be born Israelites, but all are not the chosen children, or princes of God (Deuteronomy 7:6-7, 14:2). This statement was spoken out of Paul's compassion for Israel, for he wished all of Israel were saved. He confirmed his understanding in a profound prophetical statement by the prophet Isaiah, "Though the number of the children of Israel be as the sand of the sea, a remnant shall be saved" (Romans 9:27).

In addition to the commandments of God to Israel, Moses wrote the reasons why God wanted Israel to walk holy among other nations. He explained that God had not set his love upon them, nor selected them because they were more in number than any people, for they were the fewest of all people (Deuteronomy 7:7). In any place or situation, and among any people, the chosen of God are sanctified by God's will, and not by what they have done or how great they are. God loves His people and He will keep His promises made to the patriarchs of old concerning Israel and the Gentiles. The promises concerning Israel would come to pass so that God's election might stand (Romans 9:11-12).

Despite being the eldest, it was ordained that Esau would serve Jacob. God hated Esau and loved Jacob (Romans 9:13). Some people think God hated Esau because He knew Esau would reject Him. This may be true seeing only God knows the heart. According to the scriptures, God's compassion was not based on anything either of the two brothers had done, but rather, because God chooses, and has mercy on whom He will.

Esau's rejection of his birthright was secondary to the calling of God (Hebrews 12:16). He was not of Abraham's seed, which is the offspring of faith. In contrast, Jacob, despite his faults, was called Israel and listed among many witnesses for his obedience of faith.

It was God's will that Jacob take the heel of Esau, displace and supplant him, for God gave the right to Jacob. The life of Jacob, prior to God changing him and his name, was proof that God loved Jacob. This record, along with many others, compels us to praise God, because God commendeth his love toward us, in that, while we were yet sinners, Christ died for us (Romans 5:8).

God's relationship with Esau and Jacob provokes intense discussions about the election of God, or God's right and ability to choose. Many responses to this subject have resulted in claims that God is unfair because He prefers one person or nation more than another. In that, God is a just God. It is impossible for Him to be unfair. And if it were possible for Him to be unfair or impartial, that would be His right, seeing He is God.

As the Father, God has the authority to lavish His children, and to correct and chasten them. This relationship is reserved for His children. As the Almighty God, He has power to save, judge and condemn souls because all of them belong to Him. God said, "All souls are mine, the soul that sinneth it shall die." This is not the voice of the Father, because the Father chastens His children so that they will not be condemned with the world. God then is the Father of those whom He has called, chosen, and justified by Jesus Christ. His purpose is to make all those that He has called out of the world, one body, or one church in Christ.

Ishmael And Isaac

"Look unto Abraham your father, and unto Sarah that bare you: for I called him alone, and blessed him, and increased him." Isaiah 51:2

In his letters to the Christians at Rome concerning the salvation of Israel, the Apostle Paul describes the election of Israel by God, explaining emphatically that being born of the natural seed of Abraham does not make you an Israelite. But rather, they that are born of the flesh are children of the flesh, and not the children of God. The children of promise are counted as the righteous seed, as in the case of Ishmael and Isaac.

Paul's statement, "All Israel is not Israel" refers to the two natures of people that exist in the world: spiritual and natural. Ishmael and Isaac were both born of the seed of Abraham. However, one is of the flesh and one is the elect, and of the promised seed.

Israel refers to "the called of God" or "God's elect." They are a people specifically sanctified from among other nations, and their name Israel was given to Jacob by God after he wrestled with the angel of God. While Israel was a nation, the name itself denoted a spiritual relationship with God. Ishmael, Israel's brother, was not called of God but rather born in bondage. God shows us clearly that salvation is confined to those whom He sanctified from the foundation of the world, called in Isaac and justified in Jesus Christ. Not even being born an Israelite according to the flesh qualifies an individual to be called a son of God, because flesh and blood cannot inherit the kingdom of God.

Hagar, an Egyptian slave, conceived Ishmael of Abraham. He was considered a child of the flesh because he was not the son that God promised would be born of Abraham and Sarah, but rather a result of an act of impatience. Ishmael represents the carnal minded man who walks and acts according to his flesh, and who is in bondage to the law of sin and death. Isaac was the child of promise, and he and all that are called of God, have a spiritual inheritance because they are born of a free woman.

The Apostle Paul used Ishmael and Isaac to remind the Christian Israelites in Galatia not to base their righteousness from living or serving the law of Moses, because Jesus died to free them from that bondage. He also assured them that just as Ishmael was in bondage, so were they until they were liberated in Christ Jesus.

Having been set free by the blood of Christ, Christians have been rescued from the law of sin and death. Those born of the bondwoman (Ishmael) or born in sin are servants to sin. Those who have been reborn in Jesus Christ are servants of righteousness and become heirs and sons of God through adoption.

> *"Wherefore thou art no more a servant,*
> *but a son; and if a son, then an heir of*
> *God through Christ." Galatians 4:7*

Everyone born of a woman is a slave to sin or an Ishmael. The bondwoman's seed pertains to the flesh, but Christ's seed pertains to the Spirit and eternal life. "And if we are of Christ, then we are of Abraham's seed, and heirs with Christ according to the promise" (Galatians 3:29).

These are just one of several brothers in the Bible which were used to show God's election of a remnant who has been called out to worship Him and complete His purpose in the earth, like the church.

Part IV Two Churches

"These are spots in your feasts of charity, when they feast with you, feeding themselves without fear: clouds they are without water, carried about of winds; trees whose fruit withereth, without fruit, twice dead, plucked up by the roots." Jude 1:12

TRUE OR FALSE

There are two churches or assemblies living and moving in the earth: *the church*, which is the body of Christ, and *the false church*, which consists of tares. The physical building, or the house of worship, is not the church. The people who assemble to worship are the church. The building itself, which should be sanctified for God's use, is a meeting place between God and man, as the tabernacle was in Israel. Like God called Israel out of Egypt, those that are in Christ Jesus are the church or the ekklesia of God because God called them out of the world to worship Him.

When writing to the saints who gathered in various homes for worship, Paul called them churches. Sometimes he would refer to a church or an assembly in a particular city (1 Corinthians 16:19, 18.18, Revelation 2:7, 1 Thessalonians 2:14).

Every assembly in the world has a spiritual head: Jesus Christ. He is the head of the church of God and Beelzebub (Satan) is the prince of the false church (Matthew 13:39). Satan's church consists of lying prophets, false teachers, false apostles, and false brethren. These "birds" strategically flock among the saints to pervert and pluck the truth out of those who lack understanding of the Word.

The false church lures people with an alternative gospel, which uses the Holy Scriptures with a slant that is not biblical but often sensible and acceptable to the listener. These deceivers preach another gospel, which is really not another gospel, but has an appearance of truth. And being completely deluded and swept away by this false portrait of hope, some never recover from their delusions. The opportunity for saints to be deceived by false brethren is of such concern that God repeats the warning throughout the New Testament.

> *"But there were false prophets also among the people, even as there shall be false teachers among you, who privily shall bring in damnable heresies, even denying the Lord that bought them, and bring upon themselves swift destruction." 2 Peter 2:1*

Many false prophets are in the world, which explains why many are being deceived, both young and old. Although it may seem that truth is lost, God commands the light to shine in darkness. Nothing can keep the sheep from their shepherd. Even in the darkest of nights,

God will cause light to spring forth and guide the sheep into the fold. God adds souls to His kingdom through the revelation of Jesus Christ, the savior of mankind.

> *"The people that walked in darkness have seen a great light: they that dwell in the land of the shadow of death, upon them hath the light shined." Isaiah 9:2*

Nothing shall separate God from His beloved, not death, hell, nor the grave. Jesus proved His love through His death on the cross, and by willingly descending into hell. His journey into hell was to take power from it and death, as well as to preach to the lost sheep that died in faith without receiving the promise.

Although the body of Christ is made up of various members with diverse backgrounds, they share testimonies that they have come to the knowledge that Christ is their savior. Many also testify that until they received Christ, and they felt alienated in this present world. This is because before there was an awareness of God, He was speaking to the spirit of His children leading them to His church.

There is only one true church as there is only one God and one savior. The name of the savior is Jesus the Christ. However, despite the oneness of God's kingdom, there is another church, a false system at work in the world. Satan controls this church and this system. Since his fall, he has purposed to deceive as many humans as he can. His false church is based on lies and hypocrisy, and his words are enticing but do not carry the power to change or save. Anyone can join his church.

Although individuals can choose to surrender their hearts to follow Christ, they cannot join the invisible church of God by choice. There is no prayer or oath that a person can say that will guarantee his entrance into the church of God, or give him access to the throne of God. The church is not a building in the community, but a community of people built upon the knowledge of Jesus Christ. Those who are a part of the assembly are added to the church through sanctification by God's spirit and obedience to the gospel (Acts 2:47).

The church is precious to God because He purchased it with His own blood. He didn't use the blood of bullocks, turtledoves, or lambs, but He used the pure blood from the body of the only begotten Son of God.

God gave gifts to His church to nourish it until either the total body measured up to the image of Christ, or until the body moved as the head directed. These gifts are leaders, who by the spirit of God, relate the mind of God to the body of Christ. One gift was the apostles. The Apostle to the Gentiles commanded the leaders of the churches to watch and pay close attention to those among them and the church. He warned them that the wolf was coming and that he would not spare the flock. For three years, Paul never neglected to alert the brethren that false leaders would enter the churches, and rise up among them for the purpose of destroying the flock. Satan has a church, and he recruits through these apostate leaders. These leaders roam among the true church. That is why many are tossed to and fro, or wander from church to church, or withdraw altogether. Some lost souls have been enticed by members of this false church, and because they remain in sin, they are never able to come to the knowledge of the truth.

> *"For of this sort are they which creep into houses, and lead captive silly women laden with sins, led away with divers lusts." 2 Timothy 3:6*

> *"Ever learning, and never able to come to the knowledge of the truth." 2 Timothy 3:7*

> *"Now as Jannes and Jambres withstood Moses, so do these also resist the*

*truth: men of corrupt minds, reprobate
concerning the faith." 2 Timothy 3:8*

It is imperative that babes in Christ desire the sincere milk of the Word. Babes need an appetite for truth, and need to be fed with truth. When babes are fed the gospel of truth, like the man Christ Jesus, they learn to refuse false teaching. Learning to choose good and refuse evil (Isaiah 7:15). Once the sheep are satiated by the pure Word of God, it will be hard for them to swallow a generic doctrine or false gospel because their palate will have grown accustomed to the sincere Word.

The church of Satan is growing so rapidly that hell has enlarged itself to accommodate all those that follow him into everlasting darkness. If people could choose the God they wanted to serve, they would choose Jesus who loves the church and willingly gave His life to save it. On the contrary, Satan seeks to please himself alone and be worshipped exclusively. To accomplish all of his ungodly desires, he aggressively pursues opportunities to steal, kill, and destroy the church. He can try, but Satan cannot stop the will of God to redeem His people.

Amid all the spiritual chaos and confusion, the church will hear the voice of God and refuse the seductive doctrines of the wicked one. Not even death can separate the sheep from the love of God, which is made known in Jesus Christ. God guaranteed that the gates of hell could not keep Him from building His church, and He promised that no weapon formed to destroy the sheep would prosper (Isaiah 54:17, Jeremiah 1:19). In this, the body of Christ – the church, has a strong consolation. The church is comforted by the word of God reveals that by His death, Jesus was able to enter hell and deliver His sheep from the bondage of corruption and lead them into everlasting life.

GOAT AND SHEEP

Jesus Christ is the good shepherd, and He gave His life for the sheep. He was not willing that any of His sheep should perish or be condemned with the world. He wanted His sheep to repent and be converted (2 Peter 3:9). To continue His rescue mission, Jesus sent the disciples into the world to preach the gospel. First, He sent them unto the lost sheep of the house of Israel, and then unto the Gentiles (Matthew 10:6). All that believed the apostles' report concerning Jesus received power to become the sons of God. Those who heard the gospel but didn't believe on His name were goats and are condemned (John 3:18, 8:24).

The chief shepherd and bishop of our souls came into the world to lead the sheep out of the world and into the sheepfold. He is not like a hireling who works for wages. He is not like men who see the wolf coming and neglect to warn the sheep.

The shepherd's call is the gospel and the Word of God. And when He speaks, the sheep hear His voice and follow. For this reason, Jesus told the disciples to shake the dust off their feet as a testimony against those who would not receive them. In other words, 'Don't worry if you're rejected, these are not my sheep' (Matthew 10:13-15).

Jesus sent seventy disciples out to witness in specific places. If the gospel was received, then God's spirit of reconciliation would remain in that house. When the disciples uttered, "Peace be to this house," then the peace of God would remain while the message was believed. However, if the Spirit of Christ wasn't already in the house, the messenger's blessings of peace would return unto the disciples as a testimony that the dwellers of the house had rejected the gospel. The people that received the gospel of Peace did so because they were ordained to eternal life and thus believed the gospel of peace. They heard the voice of their shepherd calling.

> *"And when the Gentiles heard this, they were glad, and glorified the word of the Lord: and as many as were ordained to eternal life believed." Acts 13:48*

While the sheep follow Christ in the world, there are goats among them. The goats may look like sheep, be a hybrid of a sheep, but they are not sheep – which is inwardly.

In the kingdom of heaven, the goat and sheep appear to be of onefold because they openly call upon the name of the Lord. However, the Word of God spoken by the Shepherd puts a separation between the true worshippers and those who have a form of godliness.

Sheep are fed and follow the good Word that they may learn to refuse evil doctrines (Isaiah 7:15). They are conditioned to be satisfied with food from heaven. The goats have no problem feasting with the sheep; however, when they are unsatisfied or discontented with truth, they not only wander to get their itching ears scratched, but they also are confused by various false and seductive doctrines (Ephesians 4:14).

Wolves dressed in sheep clothing come into the fold to prey on the sheep. While the under shepherds (ministers) are not watchful, sleep, or just not aware, the wolf enters among the sheep not sparing the flock; and the goats feed themselves off of the charity of the saints having no fear. Jude called them wandering stars and brute beasts who pretend to be ministers of light while speaking swelling words to captivate and devour the sheep (2 Timothy 3:6).

Goats are sometimes revealed when they leave the congregation of the sheep, making it known that they despise the Word of truth. This division is evident because, the goats remain among the sheep for such a time, appearing as though they have truth. However, goats do not have truth. They have an appearance of truth by their association.

Besides the goats leaving the church and making it known that they don't believe in the Shepherd, the only way a goat is manifested is in the final judgement. In the final reaping when all nations are gathered before God, He will separate them one from another, as a shepherd divides his sheep from the goats. And God will also set the sheep on His right hand and the goats on the left (Matthew 25:32-33).

Despite the false shepherd's great orations and enticing words, sheep know the sound of the true shepherd. God will never let the wolves devour His sheep. Jesus said, "All that ever came before me are thieves and robbers: but the sheep did not hear them" (John 10:8). Notice that the sheep did not hear the voice of the thieves and the robbers. Although Satan has disguised himself and planted his wolves among the sheep to destroy them, the sheep will not follow them.

Satan's message is believed and embraced as truth in this world because of his deceptive alliance with the saints. This is part of his cloak. Satan appears to be a true prophet because he is associated or among true prophets. As a result, it is a challenging task for the sheep to come out from among the world and be holy. However, God has ordained some to be vessels of honor that His name might be praised.

CHOSEN VESSELS: TO HONOR AND DISHONOR

From the time that Cain slew Abel until now, the earth has been occupied by the sons of God and the sons of wrath (1 John 3:1, Ephesians 2:3). The Apostle Paul classifies these two types in the churches as vessels of honor and vessels of dishonor. One is the offspring of God, and the other is the offspring of the devil.

> *"But in a great house there are not only vessels of gold and of silver, but also of wood and of earth; and some to honour, and some to dishonour." 2 Timothy 2:20*

As in the days of the priests and Levites, when the tabernacle and vessels were anointed and sanctified for service by the sprinkling of blood, vessels of honor are ordained and sanctified unto God by the sprinkling of the blood of Jesus Christ (Hebrews 9:19-21).

> *"Moreover he sprinkled with blood both the tabernacle, and all the vessels of the ministry." Hebrews 9:21*

The church and children of God were chosen in Christ before the foundation of the world to be honorable vessels. They were not "saved" before the world was created but rather chosen to become holy vessels unto God.

> *"According as he hath chosen us in him before the foundation of the world, that we should be holy and without blame before him in love." Ephesians 1:4*

God preserves honorable vessels in Jesus Christ so that they might show His glory in the earth. These vessels of mercy were by nature the children of wrath (Ephesians 2:3). However, God predetermined them to be conformed into the image of the only begotten Son of God. Hence, they were chosen in Him.

The almighty God purposed from the beginning to have children of honor. But because Adam became a servant to sin, all were born sinners, including those God had chosen in Jesus Christ. They became sinners by their association with Adam (Romans 3:23).

God wanted a people that would walk holy in the earth — glorifying His majesty. So, God came in the face of Jesus Christ to redeem them that were under the law so that we might receive the adoption of sons. "And because ye are sons, God hath sent forth the Spirit of his son into your hearts, crying, Abba, Father. Wherefore thou art no more a servant, but a son; and if a son, then an heir of God through Christ" (Galatians 4:5-7).

The sons of God are also known throughout the Bible as: the church, the elect, the children of God, the children of the day, the kings and priests, the beloved, and more. These are the faithful vessels God has chosen. These are the sons of God that are patiently waiting in anticipation for the redemption of their bodies.

SONS AND BASTARDS

The Old Testament meaning for son is a "builder of the family name." We know from the scriptures that God created man in His image and likeness with the intention of making many more sons; and thereby building His name in the earth.

God told Adam and Eve to "be fruitful and multiply." In other words, God made man in His image, and man was commanded to produce more worshippers that would have God's image and call upon His name. However, Adam's sin separated man from God; and Adam being corrupted brought forth seed after his own kind (Genesis 5:3).

Every child born into the world inherited the sinful nature of Adam. The only hope for the atonement of man's sin would be through the seed that God testified would come and break down the serpent's seed; and this is because God would not leave Himself without a son to build His name.

The Everlasting Father sent His seed into the world, in which it traveled through many generations to reconcile God's children hidden in the field.

"For God sent not his Son into the world
to condemn the world; but that the world
through him might be saved." John 3:17

Everyone that believes on the Son of God has eternal life (John 3:15). God didn't send Christ into the world to condemn the world for sin, the world was already condemned being born from Adam. Everyone born of Adam is in sin and is at enmity with God.

The word of God so wonderfully displays that the promise of salvation would come through a Son. Yes, through the birth of the Son of God, both the Gentiles and the Jews would be saved and made one in Christ Jesus. He was the vessel made over again in the 18th chapter of the book of Jeremiah. Jesus, the second Adam, was the express image of God.

The vessel typifies flesh because Jesus partook of flesh and blood. God did not use another type of vessel like four-footed beast or fowls. God made the second son from the same lump or flesh (His own garment of redemption). God did it again, and this man was perfect. Though He was tempted like Adam, He did not sin as Adam. This man was perfect because He was begotten of the seed of God, and thus He became the builder of the family of God, instead of Adam. And through the birth of this seed, Jesus Christ, the first Adam and his wife Eve could be saved (1 Timothy 2:15).

> *"But we see Jesus, who was made a little lower than the angels for the suffering of death, crowned with glory and honour; that he by the grace of God should taste death for every man." Hebrews 2:9*

> *"For it became him, for whom are all things, and by whom are all things, in bringing many sons unto glory, to make the captain of their salvation perfect through sufferings." Hebrews 2:10*

God came into the world as a man, which made Him the begotten Son of God. He was made a little lower than angels, who are spirits and not flesh. The Son of God, who was born of the blood of God, brought hope, grace, and truth to a dying world. If anyone receives the Son and believes on His name, that individual will have the power to be a son of God too. For as many as are led by the Spirit of God, they are the sons of God (Romans 8:14).

Power to become sons of God is in the hand of the Father. He calls men unto salvation and gives them eternal life by revealing Himself through His sonship. Not all that are in the world have this privilege, for God does not reveal Jesus Christ to everyone. No man arbitrarily can come to God except the Father draws him. The Father will resurrect His children from the earth unto eternal life just as Christ rose from the dead (John 6:44).

The scriptures that spoke of a seed that would break down the serpent's seed shows us the type of sons in the earth. One son is of the woman, who bears the seed that is of faith. The other son is of that great whore, who bears the seed of the serpent (Revelation 17:1-6). Outwardly, these representatives came from their earthly father Adam; however, spiritually God is not the Father of the serpent's seed.

Mankind must be reborn to have power to call God Father, which means any son not born of God or not regenerated according to spiritual adoption is a bastard.

Any reference to God in His dealings with bastards is spiritual and not natural. It is the spiritual state or birth that testifies whether a soul is a son or a bastard. The Mosaic Law regarding bastards was to deter the children of God from fornicating with the world and non-believers. Any child born of fornication could not come into the congregation of the Lord unto the tenth generation (Deuteronomy 23:20). This is a pattern of things in heaven because in reality, many children all over the world who were are naturally born to wed and unwed parents can testify that the blood of Jesus has redeemed them.

Additionally, God chastens and corrects His children. This explains why so many people can be in the visible church, yet some live as though they are products of the Word of God and some live as though they are products of the world. The Everlasting Father doesn't discipline everyone, but as God the creator, He restrains mankind from committing all of the imaginations of their hearts, specifically when it relates to offending God or His people (Genesis 8:2, Genesis 20:6, 1 Samuel 25:26).

God's discipline is for education and instruction so that His children may learn to be holy as God the Father is holy. Therefore, if God's divine chastisement is absent from the life of an individual who is evidently sinful, God testifies that person is a bastard and not a son.

According to the scriptures, God is not speaking to or disciplining everyone in the world. While He rains mercy upon the just and the unjust, His Fatherhood is for His children alone (Matthew 5:45). The word **father** itself denotes relationship, and the word **God** denotes sovereignty. The Holy Ghost reveals that bastards are those who have no relationship with God as the Father. These children are in the world and of the world and not of the Father. They do not receive His eternal love. "For whom the Lord loveth he chasteneth, and scourgeth every son whom he receiveth" (Hebrews 12:6).

The father of bastards is the devil, he is the great imposter. He begets seed through deception and through their rejection of the truth. Bastards are born of fornication between the sons of the earth and the mother of harlots (John 8:44, Revelation 1:5). Throughout history and through many kingdoms, bastards make war with the saints (sons) until both their mother (Babylon) and their father (the devil) are eternally fallen (Revelation 14:8, 18:2). The devil's purpose of amassing children is to overthrow the family of God. His kingdom, however, shall not prevail against the body and foundation of God, which is the church. God will not allow His name to be ravaged, neither will He allow His righteousness to be ignored.

As they stand before God for judgment, many that claimed God was their father will finally be spiritually awakened, and will learn the true nature of their relationship with God. This righteous judge will testify that based on their works, they are children of the devil. These poor souls will have to endure great torment knowing fully and clearly, that they were used as instruments of unrighteousness; and that they were deceived by the doctrines of devils and the seduction of evil spirits.

> *"For such are false apostles, deceitful workers, transforming themselves into the apostles of Christ." 2 Corinthians 11:13*

> *"And no marvel; for Satan himself is transformed into an angel of light." 2 Corinthians 11:14*

> *"Therefore it is no great thing if his ministers also be transformed as the ministers of righteousness; whose end shall be according to their works." 2 Corinthians 11:15*

Everyone working under false pretenses is of their father, the wicked one. He is the father of lies and cannot abide in truth, just like his offspring who is being deceived and deceiving others (2 Timothy 3:13). Some people don't realize they are working in iniquity. They are zealous and believe that God is their motivation, as the Apostle Paul believed before he was converted

(Acts 7:58; 8:1-3; 9:1; 22:3-16). Nevertheless, whether sin is worked ignorantly or willingly, every soul that continues to live in it shall die. God neither winks at nor excuses ignorance. He demands that all souls repent and be converted.

In the absence of peace, there is confusion, chaos, and impending death. Anyone not at peace with themselves and God are in danger of the second death — from which there is no salvation. Knowing this, everyone should strive to know whether God is their father and if they have the faith of Jesus Christ because, everyone do not have faith (2 Thessalonians 3:2).

God is the creator of all, not the Father of all. Out of compassion to save souls from eternal damnation, many have proclaimed that God is the Father of all. Despite their sincerity and love for humanity, this is not true. Jesus is the only begotten Son of God, and those that are in Christ are begotten through the spiritual adoption of sons (Romans 8:14-17). The only begotten Son of God came through the lineage of men and women that God deliberately chose and ordained, and they were of the righteous seed of Christ.

It is clear in the scriptures who the church is comprised of: both Jew and Gentile, and both male and female. Jesus fulfilled all righteousness spiritually and legally. He became the eternal High Priest through the seed of Abraham. He was in the earthly priesthood through the lineage of Mary and Joseph. Matthew's genealogy shows the birth of the begotten Son of God, and Luke's genealogy shows the birth of the appointed sons of God.

In the scriptures, all things being created by God show ownership, for God created all things including good and evil (Isaiah 45:7). All things created by Jesus Christ, who is the Son of God, reveals the creative power of God, the relationship between God and Jesus Christ, and the manifestation of God in the beginning of creation (Ephesians 3:9).

The Word was God in creation and the Son of God in re-creation or regeneration. John testified saying, "And the Word was made flesh and dwelled among us," thus showing that God always worked by and through His Word.

> *"To wit, that God was in Christ, reconciling the world unto himself, not imputing their trespasses unto them; and hath committed unto us the word of reconciliation." 2 Corinthians 5:19*

Jesus (the seed) died and was planted in the earth (the grave) to bring forth much fruit. The fruit of God is the many sons and daughters that He foreknew and ordained to believe on Him as well as manifest His name in the earth.

> *"Wherefore come out from among them, and be ye separate, saith the Lord, and touch not the unclean thing; and I will receive you." 2 Corinthians 6:17*

> *"And will be a Father unto you, and ye shall be my sons and daughters, saith the Lord Almighty." 2 Corinthians 6:18*

Jesus calling the church sons and daughters shows the relationship between mankind and God. When He calls the church "brethren," it denotes the relationship between the only begotten Son of God and those whom God has determined are sons and daughters. The proof of this relationship between Christ and God's children is, that those that Christ came to save are, "Heirs together of the grace of life" and "Joint heirs with Christ;" and therefore, they are brethren.

SAVED AND UNSAVED

"Saved" in the New Testament refers to a soul being delivered from sin and rescued from the wrath of God to come against the ungodly (Matthew 1:21, Romans 5:9, 1 Thessalonians 5:9). Through the revelation of the doctrine of salvation and the parables, it is understood that there are two types of people in the field: one is *saved* and the other is *unsaved*. One is rescued and justified (saved) while the other is condemned to inherit the wrath of God (unsaved).

At the time of Jesus' return to redeem His saints from this world, some who are in the visible church will be left. Until that day, those who are saved and delivered from sin will remain faithful and rejoice in anticipation without fear of wrath. They are fully persuaded that they are in Christ and nothing can separate them from the love of God (Romans 8:30-39).

Salvation is a process completed by God in His people, His purchased possessions. What a man does, did, or will do, cannot save them, they have no power to save (Ephesians 2:8, Titus 3:5). Man is dead in sin, and dead men cannot revive themselves. The sanctification process is misinterpreted to believe we work to be saved, not so. According to scripture, we are to work out our salvation, not work for salvation. Salvation comes through being led and sanctified by God's Spirit (Philippians 2:12-13). Like Noah, saints work by faith and obedience. This is the response to the call of God unto salvation. The saint's works prove they believe in God, and are persuaded to follow their master.

The word of God, and the works of them that are called unto salvation, prove what is acceptable unto the Lord. Saints don't work to earn deliverance from sin, but they do what is required of those that are delivered from sin. How can a drowning man save himself? Likewise, children of God work to honor the one who saved them from drowning. In keeping themselves unspotted from the world, they are a witness to God's mighty power to save and His unexplainable ability to keep those who have been rescued.

When people are regenerated, their souls are redeemed from the bondage of sin and death. As a result, they escape the wrath of God that will come on the unrighteous. Although their souls are saved, their bodies must be saved or changed to match the glorious resurrected body of Jesus Christ (Romans 8:23, 1 Corinthians 15:53, Philippians 3:21).

Man cannot work hard enough to gain eternal life. That is why the scriptures record eternal life as a gift.

When people receive the Spirit of Christ, they have that gift abiding in them. Having that eternal gift motivates believers to please God who is the giver of eternal life (Philippians 2:13); and who will change our mortal bodies, giving us body that can withstand the elements of the third heaven or abode of the Almighty God.

The sin that Jesus came to save mankind from is the imputed sin of Adam under which the entire human family was condemned (Romans 5:12). When an individual is born again, he is delivered from Adam's sin and begins to go through the process of sanctification, which is separation from the sinful nature. If a person continually sins after being regenerated, a sincere self-examination should be made to see if he or she is grounded in the faith of Jesus Christ. Those who are born of God do not practice sin. In this faith, man has to reckon himself dead to sin and alive unto God. When saints commit sin, they are compelled to repent because the seed of God is in them to convict them of their transgression (1 John 2:1; 3:4-9).

> *"The LORD of hosts hath sworn, saying,*
> *Surely as I have thought, so shall it come*
> *to pass; and as I have purposed, so shall*
> *it stand." Isaiah 14:24*

God will finish every work that He starts, which includes the salvation of man that He purposed from the beginning. Though man was lost and sold to sin by the disobedience of Adam, they would be found and redeemed by Jesus Christ. In this eternal work, the called of God are delivered from the wrath to come.

The work has to be eternal because the wrath of God is against ungodliness, which carries with its eternal consequences. When a child of God commits and act of sin after coming to Christ, that child is chastened to repent. And if that child accepts and endures the chastening, he or she will be forgiven. Why? Every child of God has an advocate with the Father, who is Jesus Christ. Every child of God must bring forth fruit or be in danger of being cut off. This is a type of purging. So, the Father's children must endure chastening, or be in danger of purging.

> *"I am the vine, ye are the branches: He that abideth in me, and I in him, the same bringeth forth much fruit: for without me ye can do nothing." John 15:5*

> *"If a man abide not in me, he is cast forth as a branch, and is withered; and*

men gather them, and cast them into the
fire, and they are burned." John 15:6

Everyone that is saved is a part of the body of Christ, they are the branches. The fruit of every tree grows on the branches. Those that are saved have a responsibility to examine themselves and mortify the sinful deeds of the flesh. The conviction will come from the Holy Spirit of God (Romans 8:13, Colossians 3:5). It's better to purge yourself then to have God the Father purge you.

All souls belong to God, however, some souls are destined or ordained to eternal damnation in the lake of fire (Ezekiel 18:4). Every 'saved' individual will escape eternal damnation. We examine ourselves to ensure we escape this wrath. We may not know the end of others – but we should know our end! Only God, who is the righteous judge, knows and determines the eternal end of an individual. Man judges from the outward appearance of things, but God knows the heart and judges the heart.

There are two kinds of people in the world. If salvation were determined by men, the innocent may perish with the guilty. To keep the innocent from being falsely marked for the lake of fire, God allows the bad seed to grow up with the good seed; and the saved to mature with the unsaved. He will do the separating in the end.

To make sure you are on the right side of God during the separation, you must be in Jesus Christ. Every soul that is in Christ Jesus at the time of the rapture will be changed; and inherit eternal life (Matthew 25:46). Those who are saved are in the world but not of this world because their lives are hidden in Christ Jesus. So the, 'saved,' sons of God will be manifested at the catching away of the church (Romans 8:19, 1 John 3:2).

Believers who have been saved from wrath are in the world, but NOT of the world. In the world believers experience the same tribulation as others do, because they are in the world. However, believers can have peace in tribulation; and they have a strong consolation in Christ, who prayed for them. The scriptures testify Jesus said, "I pray for them, I pray not for the world" (John 17:9). In this scripture, Jesus emphatically expresses God's compassion on His own and not the entire world or cosmos.

"They are not of the world" can only mean that the church or the body of Christ exists among men. Just as God let the light remain in darkness, those that have been saved from the wrath to come, are kept in the world. All things are kept by the power of God, including those who are saved or made free from the bondage of sin. All of God's will comes to pass and those who have been saved cannot be plucked out of His hand (John 10:28).

God's election to save is not based upon anything that a person has done, whether good or bad, because the selection process was completed before birth of the people. This was illustrated in Moses' writings to the Israelites as well as Paul's letter to the Romans.

> *"The LORD did not set his love upon you, nor choose you, because ye were more in number than any people; for ye were the fewest of all people."*
> *Deuteronomy 7:7*

> *"Even so then at this present time also there is a remnant according to the election of grace." Romans 11:5*

This is what Paul was trying to explain to the church in Rome (Romans 9). God will save a remnant of Israel and the Gentiles, according to election. Israel was blinded for a season to save a chosen remnant of the Gentiles. God turning to the Gentiles to save them does leave Israel abandoned. God saved many Gentiles and will not cast off Israel forever. He loves them with an everlasting love.

Having the ability to choose does not mean we have power to choose to be saved. We don't have a choice whether we will be saved, for it is God who chooses and works in us to do His will. God initiates the relationship between Himself and mankind.

The desire to be free from sin is given by God and comes when an individual is aware of their sinful condition. Jesus declared to the disciples, "Ye have not chosen me, but I have chosen you, and ordained you..." (John 15:16). The knowledge of repentance is also given by revelation. When we come to God, it is by the moving of God's spirit upon our hearts. His invitation makes us uncomfortable, and our soul becomes restless and unsatisfied until it seeks God out and finds Him.

God developed the salvation plan before creation, and His plan was performed or carried out by and through Christ Jesus. We cannot question the things God has done to save mankind because, God is sovereign and just, and His will shall come to pass (Romans 9:11-20, 28).

God is not like man, all His ways are perfect. If there are two in the field, then those who God took, He prepared to take – it was in His plan. The souls that

God left in the world, He planned to leave there and they prepared to stay. No word proceeding from God's mouth will ever fail – it will accomplish what it was spoken to perform.

The souls called out of this world by God are saved when they humbly receive and obey the gospel when it preached. When these souls receive message of Christ they are changed because, He is eternal life – He is the message of hope (John 6:54; 10:28; 17:2, 1 John 5:11-13).

Everything that receives the word of God is changed, and becomes what God has spoken. The same word that spoke in the beginning and created all living things, is the same word John said was in the beginning with God; and the word is God. God, He speaks and life appears! So, when God spoke over Mary's womb, that word became the man Christ Jesus. Then when the man, which is the living word, was planted in the earth, He became the author of eternal salvation. By this same method of planting and watering, humankind can changed and bring forth fruit unto righteous.

As Noah was called by God to enter the Ark of safety to escape the flood, God has called and saved many in Jesus Christ; and being saved, they escape the condemnation that is in the world (Romans 8:1). God sends warning before destruction and all the earth is a witness. God gives His children access to divine protection from His wrath, and there is always one door of escape, for there is only one God and He is God alone. There was only one door of escape for Noah as there will be only one for the remaining generations. That door of salvation is revealed to those who are ordained to eternal life.

The way to eternal life is through Jesus Christ. To obtain eternal life, believers must partake of His body and His blood because, He was the offering God ordained to atone for the sin of mankind. Both the body and the blood come from God, and believers partake of this sacrifice initially through water baptism in His name. Once believers are buried in a watery grave with the sacrifice, they continue commemorating this death through communion. What is the name of the sacrifice? Of course, it is Jesus. The name of Jesus is the door. It's so clear that people overlook and even dismiss it. Anyone who believes and is baptized in that name shall be saved, including those that will call on Him during the great tribulation (John 20:31, 1 John 5:53).

> *"But these are written that you may [1] believe that Jesus is the Christ, the Son of God, and that by believing you may have life in his name." John 20:31*

During these deceptive times—which are the last times according to John — there are many people claiming to be saved, and there are people all over the world professing to have a relationship with Jesus Christ. However, God said that when some appear before him in judgment, He will cast them into the lake of fire because He never knew them (Matthew 7:23). So, if God doesn't know or have a relationship with many of the people professing to be Christians, why do they continue to work in His name? The answer is, they are deceived.

Being saved by God is the best thing that can ever happen to a person. Why? When God saves, He not only rescues them from sin, He establishes an eternal relationship of peace with them; and they are reconciled to God.

Too many people are not reconciled after hearing the gospel. The revelation of how people receive the gospel is in the parable of the sower and seed. Each heart is a type of soil and the seed is the word of God. According to the parable, there are several reasons why God's message does not take root in the hearts of people.

It is possible for people to hear the truth of God and remain unchanged by what they hear. You may count various reasons why the word does not take root in the heart of people that clearly heard the gospel, however, the end results will always be two, saved and unsaved. The one that received the word on good ground, and one that did not bring forth any fruit.

It's enlightening to witness people changed through the power of the preached gospel. This is the reason many men and women go into ministry. When people accept the call and are born again everyone rejoices, including the angelic host. However, what about those that don't accept the message? Individuals cannot be saved if they reject the message. Unbelief is detrimental to anyone desiring a spiritual change. Faith is needed to see and understand God, who is Light – in Him there is no darkness (1 John 1:5)

"But if our gospel be hid, it is hid to them that are lost." 2 Corinthians 4:3

"In whom the god of this world hath blinded the minds of them which believe not, lest the light of the glorious gospel of Christ, who is the image of God, should shine unto them." 2 Corinthians 4:4

Although God is sovereign and does what He pleases (Isaiah 46:10), He is just, He won't do anything contrary to His own word. God's people are in a world that is condemned to perish because of sin. To save His people, God had to buy them back according to the laws of redemption (Leviticus 25, Jeremiah 32:6). Those that are redeemed are born again according to the scriptures. Some will believe and saved, having no understanding of what salvation is all about. They will be saved by faith, through their obedience to the gospel. Believing is a prerequisite to be delivered from sin, understand the process comes later.

The law of redemption gives the next of kin right to purchase property or inheritance lost by the previous owner. In the book of Revelation, after John was caught up to heaven John wept. He was crying because it appeared there was no one worthy to open the book with the seven seals (Revelation 5:1-10). Then came God in the flesh! He sacrificed His life, died and rose again. He prevailed, and was able to loose the seals and open the book. Yes, Jesus was God in flesh. The angels proclaimed the news of His coming and revealed His name. In Him was life, and the life was the light of men (John 1:4).

LIGHT AND DARKNESS

In the book of Genesis, in the creation of the heavens and the earth, God describes the state of man after the fall, and the process of man's regeneration. Scholars who have studied the creation of man might be astounded to find a type of the degeneration and regeneration of mankind hidden in the creation of the heavens and the earth.

> *"And the earth was without form, and void; and darkness was upon the face of the deep. And the Spirit of God moved upon the face of the waters." Genesis 1:2*

As in the beginning when the earth was without form and void and filled with darkness, man was without God. Satan had marred man while God was in the process of making him, and forming man into His image. The devastation of sin put mankind into a state that man could not escape from their own strength. God, in His inexplicable kindness, created a plan that made it possible for heavens and the earth to be regenerated, and mankind also.

> *"And God said, Let there be light: and there was light. And God saw the light,*

that it was good: and God divided the
light from the darkness." Genesis 1:3-4

Notice in Genesis 1:3-4, God does not remove darkness when His spirit moves upon the world. On the contrary, by His Word, light is spoken into the darkness and then His spirit separates them both. Therefore, by the power of God, light and darkness remain coexistent in the world, but God declares that the light is good.

By the spirit and observation of the wonderful creation of God, we can see that the people in the world are separated by the Spirit of God and truth, because God's Word and Spirit are truth. (John 14:17). These two races are the children of light and the children of darkness. The light is of God and the darkness is of this world. Each class is in the world, yet the children of light are not of the world and not of darkness, but they are a nation apart and called out of darkness.

"And the lord commended the unjust
steward, because he had done wisely:
for the children of this world are in their
generation wiser than the children of
light." Luke 16:8

The world labels people and nations of different colors and geographic locations. Their label distinguishes them as another race of people, and the extent of their alienation is based on their ethnicity. This variance is a result of sin because in the beginning, the entire earth was of one language and one speech (Genesis 11:1). There was only one race of people, the human race, and they were one under the heavens and in the eyes of God.

The language that the one people shared was from God, which He gave to Adam and those after him. At that time, the notable differences in man reflected the beauty and splendor of God. After God was made sorry, by the increasing wickedness of man, He confused the language of people and caused them to scatter in the earth.

While the world focuses on race to justify their wicked intentions, God recognizes only two races: those that walk in darkness and those that are in the light; otherwise known as the family of the earth and the family of God. Those that sit in darkness yet belong to God are called out, regenerated, and have a heavenly language. These people are joined together and have fellowship in the family of God by one Spirit, and because the blood of the lamb atoned for sin, they have a new song of redemption (Isaiah 9:2, Luke 1:79).

God called the children of light out of the children of disobedience, who walk according to their own mind (Ephesians 2:1-5). The called are the lost sheep that hear His voice, obey what they hear, and are translated into the kingdom of His dear son (Colossians 1:13); and God would make them a kind of firstfruits. These sheep are the children of light as well as the children of the day. And those who have been regenerated are neither of the night nor of darkness (1 Thessalonians 5:5).

There are two in the field, which is the world. They live and breathe together, eat and work alongside each other, and sleep and rise together. Although both enter this life walking in utter darkness, one of the two will awaken to righteousness and obey the voice of truth, while the other continues to wander in darkness.

Just as the light of God remained in darkness in the beginning of creation, God left the church in the world to be a beacon for lost souls. Those that behold the light, which shines through the glorious gospel, will have fellowship one with another and will become the light of the world. These are a people reborn of that one spirit which is God, and are shaped into the image of the only begotten Son, Jesus Christ.

"For by one Spirit are we all baptized into one body, whether we be Jews or Gentiles, whether we be bond or free; and have been all made to drink into one Spirit." 1 Corinthians 12:1

Part V Two in the Field

"Then shall two be in the field; the one shall be taken, and the other left." Matthew 24:40

ONE TAKEN AND ONE LEFT

Have you ever questioned yourself about things Jesus said in Matthew 24? Do you wonder who God was referring to in Matthew 24 when He said, "One shall be taken, and the other left?"

Many of us were taught that Jesus was referring to the rapture of the church, and that the one taken referred to believers, and the one left referred to unbelievers. The phrase "two in the field" was borrowed from a parable of our Lord and applied in the previous chapters to help illustrate the two types of people that makeup this generation. It is important to know that in the parable, those taken are not referring to the church.

"One shall be taken" is most widely believed to be the church because in similar events in the Bible, being "taken" was a good thing. For example, Enoch walked with God and disappeared because God had taken him. Elijah was taken up by a whirlwind into heaven; and if we remain faithful, we shall be taken by the Lord in the air to be with the Him eternally (Genesis 5:24, 2 Kings 2:11, 1 Thessalonians 4:17).

So, many references to being "taken" are marvelous, and most always refer to the righteous. Therefore, in God's discourse with the disciples in Matthew 24, many assume the people "taken" to be the church. The catching away of the saints and the end of the world are separate events. To fully understand who was taken and who was left in the 24th chapter of Matthew, we have to discern the times that Jesus was describing.

"What shall be the sign of thy coming, and of the end of the world?" These are the questions that the disciples asked Jesus after they marveled at the buildings in the temple at Jerusalem. The 24th chapter of Matthew records the Lord's response to that question. He responded so the disciples would not be deceived by putting their trust in the physical temple during the end time (Matthew 24:3).

When the disciples understood the temple at Jerusalem would be destroyed, they wanted to know when it would happen. So, Jesus began giving them signs of His coming and the end of the world. He further told them that no person in heaven or earth knew the time when Jesus would return, only God knew the actual time of Christ's return (Matthew 24:36).

The day and hour of the Lord's return is secret. No spiritual or natural being knows except for God the Father; however, the Spirit reveals secret things by the scriptures so the sons of God will know that that time is near; and these signs point to the end of the world and Christ's coming, which will occur simultaneously. Understanding this, when Jesus goes on to explain how there will be two in the field, it is not the time of the rapture as some have believed and been taught. On the contrary, this "taken" is a different time; it is at the end of the entire world and the end of the kingdoms of this world.

Examples of two in the field can be applied to several people in the bible (Cain and Abel, Esau and Jacob, and fleshly man and spiritual man). Only, in this parable the timing must be right to understand who the two are. In this parable, Jesus was talking about the end of the world. Matthew clearly shows you what time Jesus was referring to, and Luke shows you clearly who was taken.

> *"For wheresoever the carcase is, there will the eagles be gathered together."* Matthew 24:28

> *"Immediately after the tribulation of those days shall the sun be darkened, and the moon shall not give her light, and the stars shall fall from heaven, and the powers of the heavens shall be shaken:"* Matthew 24:29

Jesus responded to the disciples questions, which started with a warning not to be deceived; and ended with what time period people would be in when two are in the field and one would be taken and another would be left.

One will be taken and another will be left during great tribulation. How do we know? Jesus said, "Immediately after the tribulation of those days shall the sun be darkened, and the moon shall not give her light." (Matthew 24:29). "Immediately after the tribulation." When Jesus was talking about two in the field, it was during great tribulation. So we know it was not the rapture. The rapture is prior to great tribulation.

So we know the time period of the parable. It was the end of the world, which is what the disciples asked Jesus. Jesus answered the three-part question. They wanted to know when the temple would be destroyed, they wanted a sign that He was coming, and when was the end of the world; and all referred to the Jews – not the church. Luke confirms who the people are in his record of Jesus' parable.

> "I tell you, in that night there shall be two men in one bed; the one shall be taken, and the other shall be left" Luke 17:34

"Two women shall be grinding together; the one shall be taken, and the other left." Luke 17:35

"Two men shall be in the field; the one shall be taken, and the other left." Luke 17:36

"And they answered and said unto him, Where, Lord? And he said unto them, Wheresoever the body is, thither will the eagles be gathered together." Luke 17:37

If you focus on the time Jesus was referring to, you can see Jesus's answer to the question in Luke 17:37, "Where Lord?"

Here is the understanding based on Luke's testimony: There shall be two people in the field, which is the world. The two people are doing the same thing during the great tribulation and the end of the world. It's nighttime. It not important what they're doing, but what happens to them and how they respond. Whether it's a man or woman, or whether they are working in the grinding mill or sitting on a couch. The disciples wanted to know what happed to a specific group of people in Jesus' parable. Let's look at the question again to see which group Jesus was talking about in His answer to them.

> *"And they answered and said unto him,*
> *Where, Lord? And he said unto them,*
> *Wheresoever the body is, thither will the*
> *eagles be gathered together." Luke 17:37*

There were two in the field. One is taken and the other is left. Which group was the disciple's concerned about? Those that were taken. How do we know? Well, look again, you already know where the people were left. One is left at the grinding mill, one left in the field, and one is left on the bed (couch). So, if you know where everyone is left, what would be your question after reading Luke 17:345-37. You would ask about those taken. That's what the disciples were asking, "Where Lord?" Where were they taken? Jesus told them, "Wheresoever the body is, thither will the eagles be gathered together."

So how do we know this this is NOT the rapture? Well Luke said, "Wheresoever the body is," that's where the eagles will be gathered. Just in case your mind thought that was a good thing, look at Matthew's account of the same verse.

"For wheresoever the carcase is, there
will the eagles be gathered together."
Matthew 24:28

Do you see the difference? Matthew said, "Carcase."
So Jesus wasn't referring to a group of bodies as if
there was a rapture or catching away of the saints. No.
This was a horrific event — Jesus was referring to
dead people. And how you know where the bodies were
taken is to look for the gathering of eagles.

This was during great tribulation and the day of
the Lord vengeance. This is the time when Jesus told
the disciples to flee to the mountains. If you are on the
rooftop... don't go back in the house. Jesus even gave
them an understanding of when they were supposed to
flee to the mountains (Luke 17:31).

"When ye therefore shall see the
abomination of desolation, spoken
of by Daniel the prophet, stand in the
holy place, (whoso readeth, let him
understand:)" Matthew 24:15

"But when ye shall see the abomination
of desolation, spoken of by Daniel the
prophet, standing where it ought not,

(let him that readeth understand,) then let them that be in Judaea flee to the mountains:" Mark 13:14

Both Matthew and Mark record the act or event that is a sign for the Jews to flee to the mountains. They are to flee because the wrath of God is coming upon the world.

The abomination of desolation, or the abomination that brings desolation; this is when the antichrist sits down in the holy place in the temple at Jerusalem. When He calls himself god, that is a sign for God people to flee from the wrath of God.

"And from the time that the daily sacrifice shall be taken away, and the abomination that maketh desolate set up, there shall be a thousand two hundred and ninety days." Daniel 12:11

Daniel's record shows the time period and the event that precedes the day of the Lord. A thousand two hundred and ninety days is equal to three and half years, which is great tribulation. The great tribulation is not like common tribulation that mankind goes through just for being born into the world. No. This is trouble like no man or woman has ever know or witnessed. And it starts with God giving the antichrist an army and them treading on Jerusalem.

> *"But the court which is without the temple leave out, and measure it not; for it is given unto the Gentiles: and the holy city shall they tread under foot forty and two months." Revelation 11:2*

This is great tribulation, "Forty and two months," is equal to three and half years. God will give the antichrist and army to trouble the Jews. He will start by taking away their sacrifices – stopping them, and then he will take a seat in the holy place.

> *"And when ye shall see Jerusalem compassed with armies, then know that the desolation thereof is nigh." Luke 21:20*

So Jesus gave the Jews a sign when great tribulation was near, and what causes the abomination of desolation, and when the day of the Lord's vengeance starts. The signs are to save the remnant of Israel. Every that believes in the word of the Lord will flee as He instructed and all others will die and become food. When will this happen? The day the Lord returns for vengeance.

"And he hath on his vesture and on his thigh a name written, King Of Kings, And Lord Of Lords." Revelation 19:16

"And I saw an angel standing in the sun; and he cried with a loud voice, saying to all the fowls that fly in the midst of heaven, Come and gather yourselves together unto the supper of the great God;" Revelation 19:17

"That ye may eat the flesh of kings, and the flesh of captains, and the flesh of mighty men, and the flesh of horses, and of them that sit on them, and the flesh of all men, both free and bond, both small and great." Revelation 19:18

There will be two in the field during the great tribulation; two types of people in the earth, those that believe in the Lord, and those who have rejected Him. It's the same in every bible situation, whether it is light and darkness, or day and night, or saved and unsaved. I pray every reader is on the right side, then you will escape all these things that shall come upon the world. I hope to see you in the new heavens, with our Lord.

"But the day of the Lord will come as a thief in the night; in the which the heavens shall pass away with a great noise, and the elements shall melt with fervent heat, the earth also and the works that are therein shall be burned up." 2 Peter 3:10

"Seeing then that all these things shall be dissolved, what manner of persons ought ye to be in all holy conversation and godliness," 2 Peter 3:11

"Looking for and hasting unto the coming of the day of God, wherein the heavens being on fire shall be dissolved, and the elements shall melt with fervent heat?" 2 Peter 3:12

"Nevertheless we, according to his promise, look for new heavens and a new earth, wherein dwelleth righteousness." 2 Peter 3:13

Index

ABOUT THE AUTHOR

The author was born in Philadelphia, PA to a father who gave her a love for singing and a mother who sparked her love for words; and she found a new love after a phone call to go to California.

November 5, 1978 the author arrived in California after a dangerous bus trip; and that day God gave her glimpses of spirits that work in darkness through people. Fear drove her to find a church, and on April 22, 1979 she was saved, and found her new love.

Vivian became a lover of God and His Word at age 18, preaching her first message at age 20. She earned a BA in pastoral ministry from Aenon Bible College, Indianapolis, IN in 2005.

In addition to writing adult Sunday School literature for over twenty years, the author published two articles in the Christian Outlook Magazine, Tragic to Triumphant and Pictures of Grace.

The author is pastor of Strong Tower Apostolic Community Church in Moreno Valley, CA, a church founded March 1999 by her husband of 39 years. They are humble parents of three adult children who all are college graduates, married, and working in ministry.

She strongly believes in feeding the flock of God, maintaining a strong benevolent and spiritual presence in the community, and continuing steadfastly in the apostle's doctrine despite the changing times, "For there is no restraint to the Lord to save by many or by few." (1 Samuel 14:6)

Printed in the United States
By Bookmasters